Paradoxes of
Education in a
Republic

Paradoxes of Education in a Republic

Eva T. H. Brann

The University of Chicago Press

Chicago and London

The University of Chicago Press, Chicago 60637
The University of Chicago Press, Ltd., London

© 1979 by The University of Chicago
All rights reserved. Published 1979
Paperback edition 1989
Printed in the United States of America
98 97 96 95 94 93 92 91 90 89   6 5 4 3 2

Library of Congress Cataloging in Publication Data

Brann, Eva T. H.
    Paradoxes of education in a republic.

    Includes bibliographical references and index.
    1. Education—United States.   2. Education and
state—United States.   3. Education, Humanistic—
United States.   4. Education—Philosophy.   I. Title.
LA209.2.B73   370'.973   78–10228
ISBN 0–226–07135–9
ISBN 0–226–07136–7 (pbk.)

Contents

1

Introduction

THE INTENT OF THIS INQUIRY

A certain uneasiness of the intellect arises when, in respect to an important matter, almost too much has been uttered, though something more might yet be said. This uneasiness induces an ambition to find more telling terms for the debate. Its pursuit could hardly be called a scholarly investigation; call it, rather, a reflective inquiry.

The present inquiry arises from a recurrent sense that American education embodies certain *root dilemmas* that would become much more amenable to reflection and resolution if they were seen as originating in the very foundation of this country. I shall therefore articulate several paradoxes of education in a republic in general and of the early American Republic in particular in order to recover the roots in thought—and quite incidentally, in time—of some familiar practical perplexities in American education.

By a *paradox* I do not mean a want of self-consistency in popular opinion about a subject, but a dilemma inherent in the thing itself, the kind of inner breach not improperly called tragic, a grave difficulty that enhances rather than degrades its matter. Therefore I mean to omit almost

* This work was written while I was a Fellow of the Woodrow Wilson International Center for Scholars, but it was conceived in the course of a score of years' teaching at St. John's College in Annapolis, Maryland.

1

all consideration of the usual circumstantial difficulties of education.

Among these latter there are, first, those inconvenient and unalterable facts of human nature which make education a perennial struggle, for example, the perverse circumstance that, just when the time is right and the intellect at its height for study, the passions are also most irrepressibly distracted. A similar human fact, with broad institutional consequences, is the evidently incorrigible disproportion between natural teachers and students capable of learning. This is a stumbling block to good education, even in aristocracies, which becomes so much the more obtrusive in democracies: "There exists now almost everywhere so exaggerated a number of institutions of higher learning, that far more teachers are continually needed for these than the nature of a people, even if richly endowed, can bring forth." (Nietzsche, *The Future of Our Educational Institutions*, Third Lecture.)

Next, there are those miseries and indignities which follow predictably from our ordinary human infirmities, for example, the inevitable inertia of intellect immersed in matter that governs so much of the life of learning: "For what I would, that I do not; but what I hate that do I." Then there are the debasing consequences of the fact that schools are largely eleemosynary institutions, offering at a loss goods not in raging demand, harboring artlessly greedy faculties, and guarded by administrating administrations.

And finally, I want strictly to avoid all those problems which are usually referred to an agent called *society*. I must confess right away that I think that society, viewed as a source rather than a sum of actions, is a debilitating anthropomorphism. It is debilitating because it encourages people to call for large, remote revisions instead of doing here and now some small immediate thing, and to scatter general blame without pointing precisely to the persons, possibly themselves, who are responsible and should pay. It seems to me that the social construction of educational problems, at least, is usually a futile misconstruction.

Besides, some reading in the history of education produces a recurrent sense of déjà vu; all the pedagogical miseries are so old! "Our post-revolutionary youth," wrote Jefferson to Adams, "are born under happier stars than you and I were. They acquire all learning in their mothers' womb, and bring it into the world ready-made." (5 July 1814.) Or: "They say that we learn nothing in the lectures, especially in the higher books, namely of physics and the like, but when the time comes for promotion it will be given to us." (*Scholars' Manual* at Heidelberg University, 1481.)[1] Evidently, one-and-a-half centuries ago reading was already going out of fashion and five centuries ago degrees were being degraded.

What is more, our intellectual world, although it may lack the closure needed to breed grandeur, is a world of civility and variety and industry. And our educational institutions have a significant history that roots them firmly in the Republic, a good deal of present appropriateness, and probably more resilience than we imagine. On the whole, I think, they have done no worse in this century than in the last: "If he singles out the learned, he will be astonished to find how few they are; but if he counts the ignorant, the American people will appear to be the most enlightened in the world." (Tocqueville, *Democracy in America*, I, xvii.)

Naturally, I do have some views about the relation of inquiries like mine to practice in our present situation. It seems to me that our time is not an era in which the scene of learning can teem with much newness. I believe that possibility began to vanish three centuries ago, when methods for the intentional production of novelty were instituted and *innovation* became a term of daily business. I think the external excitation and the internal feeling of dust-and-ashes with which each foray into novelty is received are indeces of this condition. Compare for instance the insipid and rehearsed mode in which modern men take possession of an arid moon with the marveling exactitude of the first relations concerning the landings in the strange New World, even by so gold-obsessed a man as Columbus—or, more to the point, the early educational writings of this Republic with the dreary "revolutions" of contemporary publication.

Our strength is not in newness anymore. I think that we

live—barring catastrophe—in a gently heaving but essentially stable country "builded as a city that is compact together." There may indeed be enormous social shifts, great revolutions of opinion, large charges in "life styles," "accelerating tendencies" this way or that. But all these phenomena of aggregation need not—do not—bring with them one genuine epiphany of newness. The educational scene mirrors the era and the country. It, too, is an enormous, compacted complex of cherished vestiges, trashed experiments, recovered truisms, partial reformations, occasional explosions, compromising accommodations, paths of least resistance, hopeful engraftings, institutional inertia. The educational main is a shoal of wrecked reports, of reports widely disseminated and minimally implemented. And the most revolutionary reforms leave the scene most diminished:

> Mountains will heave to bring forth.
> Born: a ridiculous mouse.
>
> [Horace, *Ars Poetica*, 139.]

The true motions, that is to say, competent, modest improvements, thoughtful new departures, and discriminating returns, take place within the interstices of this great stabilized heap. But such a concourse of inertial conformity and lively caprice is no system, no whole to be handled by any mortal plan. If such a complex has a directional motion at all, it is into recondite quarters quite hidden from the participants. My conjecture is that, whatever it is, it is not "forward."

It seems to me that, in this situation, writing on education should occasionally try to be practical in a way peculiarly appropriate to the matter. This is what I mean: In our time, education should be *temporally cosmopolitan* and *spatially parochial*. I shall set out in my second chapter an education that is temporally cosmopolitan: namely, a reappropriation of the tradition. By *spatially parochial* I mean that each community of learning should regard itself as the center of the intellectual world, think out its own place of education, and expect its practices to be propagated only in quickly damped waves, if at all. Whatever legitimate distinction arises will come about in such a local way, provided only it meticulously maintains the modesty of its smallness. Under this condition alone, institutional resistance to large "trends," an unwillingness always to squint at popularly "felt needs," is a privilege to be assumed with a good conscience. Of course, and even more pointedly, the effort of the single teacher is the ultimate resort of excellence in education. After all, in the matter of the spirit even a vanishingly small effect has to none a ratio of infinity.

The sort of practicality, then, that seems to me appropriate to this view of our condition is one that leaps over all manner of intermediary ratiocinations to pass from philosophy to practice. For example, all the preoccupations of the admininstrators of education and of truant teachers, such as "broad settings of priorities," "encompassing reforms of curricula," "general formulations of standards," and dozens of similar such conflations of theory and contingency, might be bypassed in favor of the arduous and crucial labor of finding benefactors for a concrete educational plan. Instead, I think, teachers should laboriously form an opinion concerning the foundations of learning and then teach accordingly—alone, if necessary, and in a community of like-minded colleagues, if they are so fortunate. In this setting the curriculum will fall out with some immediacy. Hence, the first practical activity for a teacher is not planning and projecting, but reflection. Indeed, it would seem to me almost shameful for a teacher not to be willing to bring forward such fundamental views, provided they are articulately argued and levigated with strong feelings of fallibility.

THE SOURCES USED

I have used a wide variety of works on education, some to excite thought, some to trace origins, some to support my opinions, some to define the opposition. I have supplemented these with some histories, particularly of American education.[2] Yet I, for one, would not wish to spend my life reading the run of treatises on education—nor do many others, not even the propagators of the genre themselves. Emerson, in his essay "Education," writes, "A treatise on education, a convention for education, a lecture, a system, affects us with a slight paralysis and a certain yawning of the jaws." Indeed, I have come across only one author who recommends the use of books on education in education, though that a weighty one: "Ere any flattering seducement, or vain principle seize them wandering, some easie and delightful Book of Education would be read to them." (Milton, *Of Education*.) But then, he is recommending Socratic dialogues, Plutarch, Quintilian.

What, in general, is the trouble? It stems in part from the fact that edifying speech on universally important topics is almost always semiceremonial. Certain truths, too large for falsification and too true for omission, are uttered: "Education should be as broad as man," says Emerson, truly. "The good schoolmaster is known by the number of valuable subjects he declines to teach," says another, rightly.[3] For detail, curious variations from the ordinary, termed radical, and late reversions to old wisdoms, called revolutionary, are added. Such discourses have the vital function of all ceremonial discourses: They set a public seal on a matter that marks it as pervasively important. But they rarely contain working hypotheses. One great exception I can think of is Charles Eliot's Inaugural Address at Harvard in 1869, which foreclosed the future on the required college curriculum in America.

The chief offenders in flaccid edification seem to me to be the humanists (and their modern heirs), even Erasmus and Vives.[4] Vives' *On the Transmission of the Disciplines* (1531) is full of humane pedagogy, the love of learning, still suggestive reading lists, and some powerful anticipations of modernity. But the pervading tone is set perfectly in the preface: "I reflected that there is nothing in life more beautiful than the cultivation of the mind through what we call the branches of learning [*disciplinae*], by means of which we separate ourselves from the way of life and customs of animals and are restored to humanity, and raised toward God Himself." Now these are elevating truths, but they do not have the taut grip of real reflection. The humanists believe them with genuine zeal, but their arguments always run to learnedness; they live in a world of reference rather than of reason. In the end, they voice mere opinion.

Another difficulty of our day is that works on education (like other counsels on public concerns) have no particular addressee. Formerly, such advice was addressed to a patron. Then all the obligatory obsequiousness could be confined to the dedication, and the body could contain all manner of magnificant presumption—as, for example, in Bacon's *Advancement of Learning*, dedicated to James I.[5] Present-day writers, on the other hand, must make themselves acceptable to a general reading public. Consequently, the issues must all be conceived very broadly, in terms of "our changing times," the "needs of society," "the whole system." As Tocqueville puts it, the democratic writer "perceives only the immense form of society. . . . His ideas are all either extremely minute and clear or extremely general and vague." (*Democracy in America*, II, bk. 1, xviii.) Furthermore, certain obligatory words, signals of right-mindedness, punctuate all the texts. I defy anyone to produce a present-day effusion on education that does not mean to further students' *creativity*;[6] for example, picked utterly at random out of a collection: "To create . . . is the uniquely human attribute." Now, I would have thought that that was what it was precisely not, and that to become a creator a student should not go to school but to heaven. Similarly with *values*; it is de rigueur to demand that a "sense of values" be instilled. It seems to bother few people that the subversive term *value* was given currency by Nietzsche to devalue our instilled beliefs and our received morality, so that nothing might be good in itself, but only as someone valued it.[7]

The necessity of speaking solemnly, the inheritance of humanist groundlessness, and the need to anticipate the public mind—all these together weaken contemporary educational writing, but the second of these most of all. The lack of an obligation to consider the foundations of a definite plan of education has in the course of time turned into an obligation to deny that there are such foundations and such a plan: "There is not, I believe, in education—and perhaps not in life—a quota of eternal verities, a set of invariant truths, a single quadrivium and trivium that must be taught to a young man lest he be charged with the failure to be civilized or humane."[8] A typical passage—but how deep into the well of things must anyone believe himself to have seen to pronounce the opinion that "it hath no bottom!"

Those works, on the other hand, that proved particularly

useful to this inquiry can be best reviewed by being grouped according to their kind.[9]

First, then, are those writings which inquire into the roots of human learning and therefore of teaching, chief among them, Plato's dialogue *Meno* (set in 402 B.C.), in which the question whether excellence is teachable is enlarged into an inquiry into learning and into teaching itself. Teaching is displayed as the activity of eliciting knowledge from the soul of the learner, and that very nature of things which makes such learning possible is set out in a myth, the Myth of Recollection. Another such work is Augustine's dialogue *On the Teacher* (ca. A.D. 383), in which the same topic is elevated into the question concerning significa-tion and communication (in the strict sense, that is, as making a matter common, as sharing), particularly of words. It is shown that all speaking is teaching; yet words convey and elicit noth-ing—they only arouse the interior man. The soul can respond only because it has a teacher within, Christ. Such a bald re-telling fails to do justice to these works which, each in its own way, intends to trace to their foundations the two chief elements of education, teaching and learning.

A second group is written by experienced and sagacious teachers. One such is Quintilian's *Formation of an Orator* (ca. A.D. 95), indirectly the most influential work on education in the Middle Ages and explicitly so in the Renaissance; similarly, Mulcaster's *Positions* (1581), which combines pedagogical élan with Elizabethan English to make the most captivating of all educational treatises that I know of.

Yet another kind of document is represented by the founding proposals, reports, and charters of going institutions, such as Franklin's "Proposals Relating to the Education of Youth in Pennsylvania" (1749) and, especially to my purpose, Jefferson's "Rockfish Gap Report" (1818), written in behalf of the commis-sioners appointed to fix the site of the University of Virginia. Other educational writings by Jefferson will also play a role, as central as it is problematic, for the hard-polish surface of his classical clarity hides certain dubious depths.

A fourth group of writings, very pleasant to read, are the educational utopias. They have the advantage of combining free theorizing with the invigorating discipline of imaginative realization; incidentally, they always represent a recognition of the concrete educational community as the locus of cohesive educational action. Among them are More's *Utopia* (1516), humanist in its educational aspect; Campanella's *City of the Sun* (1602), whose central temple is an astronomical teaching model; Bacon's prototypical research complex, the *New Atlantis* (1627). All of these institutions are in strict accordance with their founding fable; they are all exercises in imagining the application of educational theory. Add William Smith's very American *College of Mirania* (1753), where classical studies culminate in agriculture; the two German pedagogical provinces, Goethe's *Wilhelm Meister, Journeyman*, II (1821), which depicts a foundation endeavoring to combine self-expression with austerity, and finally Hesse's postmodern teaching order in *The Glass Bead Game*, the Castalian elite devoted to essentially frivolous formalisms.

Next there are certain dubious and even repellent but facinatingly potent works that have exercised enormous influence, some by inventing the tepid tyranny of the classroom technique, others by teaching the use of the iron fist in the velvet glove, still others by making education into a softly diffuse manipulative art. Comenius's *Great Didactic* and *Pampaedia* (1650–1660) belong among the first; in these works are to be found the then novel idea of universal education, facilitated by large lecture classes, using specially composed textbooks and audiovisual aids, subjected to standard criteria of performance, and taught by student assistants. In these amazing books also are collected all the now-hackneyed humanist notions: that the whole man is to be educated to humanity, that school is an experiment in living, and that education can change the world. Rousseau's *Émile* (1762) belongs under the second description, and Dewey's works, for instance the unusually concise *My Pedagogic Creed* (1897), to the last. This group is naturally more concerned with the training of children than with higher education.

Then there is a small spate of distinct little treatises that, on the other hand, had only a vanishingly discernible influence on educational practice. But so much the more do they contain a pure expression of opinion for the paradigm period for this inquiry—the early American Republic. Here is advice freely given to fellow citizens, untrammeled by too immediate a practical intention, at a rare moment when self-recognition and articulation could be of crucial long-range importance. Their main authors are Joel Barlow, Robert Coram, du Pont de Nemours, Samuel Knox, Samuel Harrison Smith, Noah Webster.[10]

Seventh and last are those fundamental texts which are not all in the first instance disquisitions on education, but which ground educational plans in human nature and in nature itself. First and unrivaled is Plato's *Republic* (II and VII), which articulates and orders in their philosophical and political context what later came to be known as the liberal arts. There follows the final book of Aristotle's *Politics*, which places the culmination of political craft in education; as always, the Aristotelian approach is sensible and deep at once. First of the modern works is Bacon's *Two Books of the Proficience and Advancement of Learning* (1609), the introduction to the *Instauratio Magna*, the great foundation of modern learning; it is ultimately responsible for the intellectual design of our modern institutions of higher learning. Finally, there is Locke's *Some Thoughts Concerning Education* (1693), the most pedagogically influential treatise in America, and, more explicitly philosophical, the posthumous *Of the Conduct of the Understanding*; it was intended as a chapter of the *Essay Concerning Human Understanding*, the most authoritative philosophical text at the time of the American founding.

Since in serious philosophical works the whole makes the parts, no reference to them is legitimate without at least some rudimentary total interpretation. Conversely, every interpretation must rest on precise references; it is impermissible to use texts as if they were some sort of intellectual tint: Aristotelian, Baconian, Kantian, etc.[11] I have tried to bear that in mind in my use of these texts.

DEFINITION OF TERMS

The Term Republic

It is specifically education in a republic that I want to consider. When Cicero translates the Greek title *Politeia* of Plato's work as *Res Publica*, "Republic," and defines as *res populi*, "people's property" in the Roman sense, which includes building and real estate (Cicero, *Republic* I, xxv), he catches just that concrete element which seems to me peculiar to this term. A republic is a commonwealth, public property, but with a caution, as Sir Thomas Elyot points out in his *The Book Named the Governor* (I, i), a work on the education of rulers. He wrestles with the term *republic*: It is, he says, a "public weal," "a body living," and yet not a common weal if that were to mean a polity where "everything should be to all men in common." It is rather a reified realm—it is not an abstraction—that is neither mine or thine, nor yet quite ours, but precisely *public*. It forms one living body that has no single soul or being—it is not the "State." The revealing contrary of a republic in the largest exact sense is the communion of the church, a true unified community, and of the spirit. For example, the Puritans made a spiritual covenant while yet in England, but they undertook to convenant and combine themselves "into a civil body politic" only on their arrival at Cape Cod ("Mayflower Compact," 1620).[12] By *republican* I therefore mean first of all what pertains to a peculiarly worldly public realm, something quintessentially political.

In the narrower sense, I intend the term *republic* to designate the American polity, which each Founding Father defines in accordance with his preoccupations. Jefferson insists on the democratic aspect of the Republic:

It must be acknowledged that the term *republic* is of very vague application in every language.... Were I to assign to this term a precise and definite idea, I would say, purely and simply, it means a government by its citizens in mass, acting directly and personally, according to rules established by the majority. [To Taylor, 28 May 1816.]

Adams takes the point of view of public right:

> The very definition of a republic is "an empire of laws and not of men." [*Thoughts on Government*, January 1776.]

And Madison completes the description with the specifically American element, not unsignificantly omitted by Jefferson:

> The difference ... between the American and other republics, consists in the principle of representation; which is the pivot on which the former move, and which is supposed to have been unknown to the latter, or at least to the ancient part of them. [*Federalist* No. 63.]

So *republican* means political in the highest general sense and in the specifically American case, democratic, constitutional, representative (and, not unconnectedly: closely bound up with modern science). Out of the meaning of this term arise the oppositions that make republican education problematic: worldly and reflective, public and private, elite and popular, lawful and moral, principled and practical, and many more. But all of these oppositions ultimately derive from the peculiar dual position that a republic by its very nature assigns to a citizen, a being at once an *individual*, an indivisible atomic—least and equal—constituent, and a *person*, an illimitable, spontaneous, incommensurable subject.

That the polity should determine education is an old thought: "No one disputes that when this does not happen in political communities it hurts their constitution." (Aristotle, *Politics* VIII, 1337a.) That "it is in a republican government that the whole power of education is required" was first observed for moderns by Montesquieu. (*Spirit of the Laws*, III, 3.)

There must then be a specifically republican education for members of a republic, or *citizens*, just as there are many other kinds of specific education: education for kings (Xenophon *The Upbringing of Cyrus—kyros* happens to mean *authority* in Greek); for philosopher-rulers (Plato, *Republic*, in which the education is for philosophy, the leap into the city for love); for a man of affairs (Quintilian, *Formation of an Orator*—an orator is a public man, simply); for a man of Christian faith (Augustine,

On Christian Doctrine II explains the use of pagan learning for biblical study); for a courtier (Castiglione, *The Book of the Courtier*); for a Christian king (Erasmus, *Formation of a Christian Prince*); and even, among the humanists, for a human being (as peculiar a vocation, it turns out, as any). I expect to find this specifically republican education set out in those works of the early Republic which I have already mentioned, and especially in Jefferson's writings on education.[13] These writers, and Jefferson first among them, reflected self-consciously, specifically, and largely on citizen education. To be sure, neither Jefferson's legislative proposals nor his philosophical views were either completely or wholly successfully realized in his time; nonetheless, both his intellectual and his institutional advice eventually prevailed, though there is not much definite evidence that it prevailed as identifiably his.[14] I refer to such items as secular curricula, university scholarship, elective studies, departmental organization, and a staged system of public education. For example, when in 1869 Eliot announced the institution of an elective system at Harvard, he gave no credit to its early American proponent, though he did refer to the two great sources of Jefferson's views, Bacon and Locke.[15] In other words, Jefferson had anticipated what he himself would have called the genius of the American Republic, or at least one of its expressions.

One more word in justification of the use of early American texts in this inquiry. Aristotle says that the lawgiver should see to it that political communities have educations to fit their polity; the American Founders were certainly lawgivers. Montesquieu says that education is of importance, particularly in a republic; the Founders knew and approved that argument. Consequently, they fully accepted the responsibility entailed in the ancient and the modern advice. On the other hand, it is a perennial matter of debate how much the Founding is still the foundation of American life. My assumption here is that in this country the beginning truly rules, both insofar as its consequences inform our educational institutions and insofar as it provides an ever-applicable reference. In other words, the beginning acts in our times, sometimes in the form of an unavoidable corruption, sometimes as a satisfactory consummation, sometimes as a laborious restoration, sometimes as a brave flaw writ large. To be sure, the educational views of the early writers had no wide systematic effect; the first great piece of national legislation was the Morrill Federal Land Grant Act, signed by Lincoln in 1862. For the first three generations, education was largely left to its own devices, to local enterprise, partly no doubt because the energetic government required for the institution of an educational system was precisely what at least some of the early writers actually eschewed in their larger political views— the federal Constitution notoriously contains no clause on education. These early private growths expressed an older, classical tradition in the indigenous American mode; it was on them and against them that the effects of the Founders' theory were finally projected.

The Term Education

The whole question concerning education is just this: Who should learn what so as to become what and do what, and how and by whom and with whom is it to be taught?—which question comprehends the learner, the object of learning, the transformation worked, the practical purpose, the plan of study, the teacher, and the community of learning. Perhaps one should add: With what expectation of success?

I shall contain this vast inquiry by pointing out that education is usually understood to have two aspects—one for those who administer it, properly called *teachers*—namely, those who show something (as in the cognate word *token*), and another for those who undergo it, usually called *students*, that is, those who apply themselves (from Latin *studere*). The difficulty with either activity is its elusiveness. For what is teaching? The ceremonial answer, nice but metaphorical, is to give the Latin etymology of *to educate*, namely, to lead out of—out of childhood into maturity, out of the cave into the light, out of tradition into freedom, out of potency into actuality. So let me draw on an Aristotelian articulation, not for an answer, but merely to fix the question.

He distinguishes four kinds of intelligent pursuit: knowledge, or truth beheld (*theoria*); practical wisdom or discernment in action (prudence); know-how, or rationally accountable making (*technē*); and experience, or a knack learned by trial and error (*empeiria*). (*Nicomachean Ethics* VI, 1139 b ff.; *Metaphysics* I, 980 b ff.)

Now, is teaching a kind of knowledge? Presumably, knowledge is a condition of teaching—though the greatest of all teachers proclaimed that he knew nothing (Plato *Apology* 21)—but teaching itself, although a mediation of knowledge, need not itself be knowledge. Aristotle claims that the sign of something being knowledge is that it can be taught. Although there are schools for teachers, it is doubtful that the essence of teaching can be taught.

Next, is teaching a sort of practical wisdom? The teacher's work certainly seems to share with politics that chief of all instruments of republican activity, purposeful, persuasive speech. Yet the deed done in teaching is not easily verified—it is hard to tell whether students have learned and, if they have learned, whether by reason of being taught. To teach well is certainly to act wisely on another; but, in the affairs of the intellect, the practical effects of action are practically imperceptible, at least in essential matters.

Is teaching then a craft, a learnable method for making something out of "student material"? Certainly, teacher-training at its best has the character of an apprenticeship; certainly, teachers use instruments, not least themselves, to work on the student; certainly, educational institutions are spoken of as turning out products. But this way of speech, derivative from industry, is (or ought to be) generally understood as a slightly repellent metaphor.

Is teaching then, finally, a knack? Undoubtedly, all good teachers have bags of tricks. But they have them because they are good teachers, not the converse.

The long and the short of it is that it is hard to establish even what mode of intelligent activity teaching is. Not that it is difficult to give a sensible account of what institutional teachers faithfully do—they become adequately competent in a subject matter, prepare a teaching plan, meet their classes, conduct them according to some orderly method, and have conferences with their students. But no one (except perhaps educationists) could imagine that this course of behavior makes a teacher. For my own part, I shall argue later that the etymological meaning of the word *teacher* is trustworthy—that to teach is conscientiously to *show* something, namely, the teacher's own learning, both as an acquisition and, more important, as a process.

The other aspect of education is what the student learns. What is an education, in the most pointed and most proper sense?

I think that the course of education is the course of *learning to read*, and to have an education is *to know how to read*. I mean reading in a wide sense, but I do mean reading. Education and literacy in a large sense are convertible terms. By this understanding, education is not "as broad as man." But it gains an assignable meaning.

There is a world that comes into being and moves quite without us—the world of nature. There is a realm designed and produced by us—the world of art. And there is a sphere that reflects or, perhaps, frames these two—the world of knowledge, *orbis intellectualis*.

Education is the course in which human beings learn to take up and read that reflective sphere, and through it the other worlds. It is no accident that the word for reading is so suggestive in several languages. In Greek it is *anagignōskein*, to re-know; in English *to read* is to un-riddle. The Latin *legere* means to gather, (as also in *intellect*); in Greek this same word *legein* means to speak rationally (so also *logos*, reason). My point is only that reading is always a hermeneutic business: the recovery of meaning, the reappropriation of reflection, the interpretation of speech. Therefore, reading concerns itself with what has already been thought and said. Hence, education does give access and context to original inquiry, and these acquisitions do accompany the process as a developing descant of fulfillment above the sober progress of preparation. But just as the public obligations of teaching are after all distinguishable from the private pleasures of learning, so the labor of study is not identical with the activity of thought. The daily life of even the best of schools must be a mundane mastering of other people's reflection—thought itself can be facilitated but not scheduled.

Since this reflective realm is deposited in texts, education properly centers on books—books of musical notes, of mathematical symbols, but, most of all, books of letters, words being the peculiar conveyances of thought and the most faithful way in which the gift of another's thought can be presented to us. Therefore, institutions of education are known by the quality of their book learning, and all attempts to alter that fact end either in a decline of the institution or in a counterreformation.

Now, when I call education reading, I obviously do not mean spelling and ciphering, but a more advanced literacy. The first complete curriculum, which is set out in Plato's *Republic*, is very carefully geared to age, for what will be made of a skill or a matter depends essentially on the age of the learner. So Socrates wants to withhold dialectic, the highest philosophical reflection, from the "puppies" (VII, 539) because a preparatory philosophical way (*methodos*) of studies has to be not only covered but re-covered before dialectic can be more than a playful yapping. The age for such a synoptic review of the propaedeutic studies in all their integrity is set at twenty years (537).

Until the word acquired a new meaning in modern times, this preparatory education was called by its Greek name, *encyclopaedia* (*egkyklios paideia*), literally, *the children's course in current circulation*, but often understood to mean *the all-encompassing curriculum*.[16] The course consisted of the free sciences (*eleutheriai epistēmai*, Aristotle, *Politics* VIII, 1337b), the same that were later codified into the seven liberal arts. Their content shifted, as did the institution and the age for which they were intended: monastery schools or universities; boys or young men. But whatever their intermediate employment, the guiding end was philosophy.[17]

In the New World, this classical curriculum, integral and required, devolved on the institution called *college*. It is the most long-lived and the most distinctive of American schools, with that precarious stability which characterizes typically American institutions. The kindergartens, the common schools, and certainly the universities were latecomers and, moreover, built partly on German models. The high schools, which superseded the American academies (whose most famous patron was Franklin), were shaped from above, by the requirements of the universities. But the college, with its English antecedents, had already enjoyed a good indigenous growth by revolutionary times, and it burgeoned at the time of the Founding—between 1780 and 1799, sixteen colleges (which survived) were chartered, most but not all denominational. To be sure, after the Civil War, as the universities grew and multiplied, the colleges had to yield their preeminence in higher education. But, while this new ascendancy was in the making, there took place, by way of compensation, a principled debate which, except that the terms were terser, was much like our contemporary controversy about the fate of small private colleges. The most distinguished defense was mounted by the Yale College faculty in its "Report" of 1828, and the most persuasive opposition came from Francis Wayland in his "Thoughts on the Present Collegiate System" in 1842.[18]

There is a historian's crime called "not being in step with the times," and its magnitude—indeed the fact of its commission—is revealed by decline and oblivion. In the latter half of the last century, the colleges appeared to have committed this crime, but, against expectation, they have somehow survived. In 1918, when Thorstein Veblen published *The Higher Learning in America*, a mordant review of the universities—those new scholarly empires commanded by "captains of erudition"—he concluded with a hopeful prophecy that there might be a reversion, if not to the colleges, then to the collegiate way. And such reversions have indeed been continually attempted since then, either as a return to *general education*, which usually means a broad introduction into the principal fields of research, or as a recovery of the *liberal arts*, which should mean the elementary but specific acquisition of the fundamental skills of inquiry.[19]

Now Jefferson, the most significant writer on education in the early Republic, was no great friend of the classical college—not even of his own, William and Mary, and certainly not insofar as it provided an obstacle to the founding of his university.[20] The reasons were not subtle: The college was usually sectarian, dedicated to the modest transmission rather than to the ambitious advancement and diffusion of knowledge, bound by an essentially prescientific plan of studies, and not easily integrable into a coherent system of public education. It is therefore likely that the paradoxes of American education will display themselves in a juxtaposition of Jefferson's modern plans for his state university and the conservative practices of the semiprivate colleges.

These historical considerations are, however, only the circumstantial aspect of the reason why the college is the right focus of this inquiry. More essential is the argument that it is the place where education, in the pointed sense I have given it, most naturally occurs (which sense precludes a peculiarly "higher" education in favor of education simply). For the student, the collegiate years are traditionally those between sixteen and twenty-two, late adolescence and early youth. They seem to be appointed by man and nature for a special interlude. At that moment, human beings are usually still free of family responsibility, not yet having "given hostages to fortune," and the world is willing to grant them leisure. At that same time, there occurs a felicitous conjunction of two conditions very serviceable to education. First, the intellect is particularly keen and receptive, so that the deepest and most difficult metaphysical speculations are avidly taken up and explicated then, even by people who will never again do more than remember (like a certain Antiphon in the Socratic dialogue *Parmenides* [126 c]). Second, the passions are mature enough for those serious erotic experiences to have taken place without which much of poetic and philosophic literature is a closed book—provided that affairs of love do not altogether prevent learning. (Incidentally, very similar circumstances, though in a mellower key, obtain again in late middle age, and the colleges may one day look there for students.)

What goes before is, no matter how strenuously teachers try to "make pupils think for themselves," mostly and properly a kind of training; where children are concerned, "this we call education; which is, in effect but an early custom." (Bacon, *Of Custom and Education*.) What comes after is again, properly, training; namely, graduate, professional, or practical training for adults. It is an ineradicable American tradition that the intervening collegiate episode should *not* be training but education.[21]

The Three Paradoxes: Utility, Tradition, Rationality

Now, finally, to those particular paradoxes of education in a republic which I have distinguished. They can be set out under three headings: Utility, which concerns the purposes and ends; Tradition, which concerns the means and ways; and Rationality, which concerns the content and substance of education.

The idea of *utility* is that of an instrumentality, a means. In education it refers to learning intended for a worldly use. There are corruptions and misconstructions of educational utility, but legitimate usefulness is primarily of two sorts: individual and social. The former includes vocational and professional training; the latter, citizen education. Citizen education is the principal preoccupation of early republican writers on education, preeminently of Jefferson. Implicit in their writings are certain perennial republican oppositions: Tradition—Revolution, Schooling—Life, Excellence—Equality, Citizen—Statesman, Citizen—Philosopher. Beyond all of these is the paradox of utilitarian education itself: that it treats learning, which is naturally an end in itself, as a means. The resolution is, once given a clear recognition of the difference of useful and liberal learning, to regard them as complements rather than alternatives, for *liberal education* provides that inquiry into ends which is crucially necessary to a republic congenitally engaged in instrumental activity.

The *tradition* is here taken to mean the collection of texts generally recognized as the founding books of Western learning. The Founders sometimes unwittingly and sometimes explicitly repudiated the study of this tradition as the principal means of becoming educated, although they themselves had followed that way. This rejection was not wanton, but in accordance with the secular and scientific roots of the Republic. Its chief features were the eclipse of classical learning; the preferential concern with "things, not words"; the deliberate decline of attention to texts. Yet, insight into origins is essential to a citizen, and even the nature of the Founding becomes inaccessible once the tradition is subverted. The resolution proposed is a recovery of the tradition in a specifically republican spirit. The educational enterprise proposed is not exposure or research, but inquiry—a direct, unpretentious, common pursuit of meaning. The means are *readings of original texts* of poetry, science, and philosophy, each to be justified by a particular rationale, all to be undertaken for the sake of a recovery of origins.

Rationality is a pervasive mode, endemic to the American democracy, whose chief commandment is "to seek the reason of things for oneself and in oneself alone." It has a number of related facets, each in itself problematical: The obligation to think for oneself turns everyone else's thought—and finally even one's own—into mere opinion. The compulsion for self-expression is hard to harmonize with the necessity to be objective. The discernibly different undertakings of seeking truth, that is, of being receptive to it, and of theorizing, that is, of making rational constructions, become confused. The instrumental rational tool of the self, the mind, whose last resort is self-evidence, works on an alien matter presented to it, which is construed as evidence, but the former tends to forestall reflection and the latter, immediacy. Rationality itself, located in the head, gives rise to the heart as an oppressed opponent: Mind and emotion are in their very conception at odds. Finally, the consequence of this mode in the public realm is a ubiquitous formalism, a deliberate preponderance of methods over ends, of pursuit over realization, of possibility over actuality, while a diminished content and substance are driven into the private world.

Each of these facets of rationality has all too familiar effects on education: In the strange ambition to "make" students think for themselves, in the rage for "creativity," in the attempt to "train the mind," in the call for educating "the whole person," in the urgent demand for "values."

The resolution proposed is an occasional return to another mode of learning in which the paradoxes of rationality are reconciled. It is a question-asking mode, in which instrumental reason yields to receptive intellect, theoretical construction to contemplative theory, critical delimitation to expectant openness. I call it *inquiry*.

Utility

The Various Aspects of Educational Utility

> Some one who had begun to read geometry with
> Euclid, when he had learned the first theorem,
> asked Euclid: "But what shall I get by learning
> these things?" Euclid called his boy and said:
> "Give him three cents, since he insists on making
> a profit out of what he learns."
>
> Stobaeus

> I have before mentioned mathematics, wherein
> algebra gives new helps and views to the under-
> standing. If I propose these, it is not, as I said, to
> make every man a thorough mathematician or a
> deep algebraist; but yet I think the study of them
> is of infinite use even to grown men.
>
> Locke, *Of the Conduct of the Understanding*, 7

These two passages[1] are eminently illustrative of
two most fundamentally different views of learning, because both concern mathematics, once
regarded as the essentially learnable knowledge: In
Greek, someone who is "mathematical" is literally
"one who is engaged in learning" (*mathēma*:
learning). The Euclid of the anecdote thinks it an
indignity even to voice the argument that mathematics is to be learned for its own sake, or at least
not for worldly use. That case is made most boldly
in Plato's *Republic*: "Geometrical inquiry . . .
then, will be that which draws the soul to truth and
produces a philosophical disposition for tending
upward where we now tend downward, as we ought

23

not.'' (527b.) That is, the true aim of mathematics is, by filling the soul with pure objects, to draw it to philosophy; and so it is in antiquity even for a sophist: "Gorgias the rhetorician said that those who neglect philosophy while busying themselves with the mathematical curriculum [*egkyklia mathēma*] are like the wooers who, wanting Penelope, slept with her maids.''[2]

Locke, on the other hand, regards it as training for the understanding. Mathematics, he goes on to say, will apprise the reasoning faculty of its own fallibility, enable it to distinguish and relate ideas, and give it practice in carrying through long trains of argument. It is for him a kind of mental gymnastics that trains the leading faculty of the mind to be fit and well-functioning for use in the world.

A mind, stocked like a *cabinet* through experience, engaging in *operations*, and *employed* or *used* on precisely delimited matter—these are the Lockean terms (to be considered further in the chapter on Rationality). The likening of the training of the soul to gymnastics is, to be sure, an ancient commonplace,[3] and the instrumental intelligence can, like so many important modern ideas, be traced to the Stoics. But it is not too inaccurate a synopsis to claim that the notion of *training the mind for use* belongs peculiarly to the mainstream of modernity. The two passages, therefore, represent, on the highest plane, a difference, roughly ascribable to the ancients and moderns, concerning the place of utility in education. Before I return to it at the end of the chapter, the several mundane manifestations in education of the utilitarian frame of mind must be set out.

The Notion of Utility

The *useful* in general is that which exists, not for its own sake, but for the sake of something else; it is not final but intermediate; it has the character of a means as distinguished from an end. The significance of this mode of existence is brought out best by citing a notion defined in opposition to usefulness— persons are thought of as beings that have their worth in themselves: "Rational beings are designated 'persons' because their nature indicates that they are ends in themselves, that is, things which may not be used merely as means." (Kant, *Foundations of the Metaphysics of Morals*, sec. II.)

While a person may be used by other persons only in a very restricted sense, a thing can be put to use, even "used up" as a resource. If a thing is specifically made to be an intermediary, it is a tool or a medium. A tool is that *by* which something is done (literally so, for *tool* and *do* are etymologically connected) or observed. A medium is that *through* which something is expressed. Instruments and media are the incarnations of the useful, for usefulness is primarily a mode belonging to *work*, to useful action in and on the world. Indeed, most of our activity is laborious work, activity not primarily done for its own sake. Such useful action, which uses tangible helps in the tangible world, is usually remote action, action through a distance. For example, the instrumental mode of being in the world puts a device between the human senses and the world, precluding direct touch or shutting out the immediate surroundings to bring close what is naturally remote. The earliest and, at its first discovery, most astounding such instrument is the telescope, the spyglass, a tube to which the eye is applied to bring the moon "as near at hand as if it were scarcely two terrestrial radii away"—as Galileo reports in awe (*Starry Messenger*). The printing press is the parallel first medium of expression, whose operation is, however, opposite in its effect. Through it one person's mind can be broadcast all over the globe, so that his expression is, as it were, carried away from himself and brought close to thousands he has never faced. One might say that usefulness is the mode of human action proper to extension, to space.

On the other hand, its possibility depends on the presence of purpose, thought. It is necessary for a rational being to intend or to will some result for anything to become useful. To be a means is precisely to be ultimately discounted in favor of an end. When that end is improperly established—false or forgotten—the mode of usefulness acquires a pathology.

This review of well-known understandings is intended only to bring out that aspect of usefulness which pertains to the present inquiry: that usefulness is preeminently a mediating worldly mode based on willing or wanting. Where the category of usefulness becomes central, an emphasis on pursuing, planning, procuring, producing, and on manufacturing, declaring, demonstrating, projecting—in short, on self-exertion and self-expression—is to be expected. This is the same mode of life consciously projected by the founders of modernity: "I am laboring to lay the foundation not of any sect or doctrine but of human utility and power." (Bacon, *Great Instauration*, Preface.)

When, then, the notion of usefulness is taken in an approving or appreciative sense, it is termed, in the language of the time most consciously concerned with it, *utility*. Hume, for instance, regularly uses the word in this positive sense. Utility is for him the primary origin of all the social virtues; all such virtues are essentially serviceable, as the private virtues are pleasurable. (*An Inquiry Concerning Principles of Morals*, sec. II, pt. II.) In antiquity, virtue was usually thought of as primarily a condition of the soul, a balanced way of being or of determining action. (Aristotle, *Nicomachean Ethics* II, 1106b.) But now the virtues have the modes of instrumentality. So the first virtue for Hume is Benevolence, the wish to be useful to others by gratifying their needs or desires. The most esteemed modern virtues are always wide-ranging, meddling virtues. So Jefferson criticizes the ancients for being defective in developing those virtues which teach us to "embrace with benevolence the whole of mankind." (To Rush, 21 April 1803.) "Self love is no part of morality," since "I consider our relations with others as constituting morality." Hence, "Nature has constituted *utility* to man, the standard and test of virtue." (To Law, 13 June 1814.) It follows that different circumstances "have different utilities"; virtue is relative to situation. Furthermore, where utility is made the principle of action, the end is always a conflation of "benefit, advantage, pleasure, good, or happiness, (all this in the present case comes to the same thing)." (Bentham, *Principles of Morals and Legislation*, I, iii.) For when the measure of virtue is its worldly usefulness, someone must be passively receiving worldly gratification, that is to say, pleasure. Pleasure must therefore be happiness, for happiness is the usual term for the human end per se.[4]

Such an equivocal utility is the governing notion of the Enlightenment. Humanity is regarded as a reciprocally instrumental species: Each person has the double aspect of being an end to himself and a tool for others. As in society, so with respect to nature: Nature is at once an object of the most disinterested research and of strenuous exploitation. (Hegel, *Phenomenology*, VI B ii b.) Since this Republic was founded under the aegis of the Enlightenment, this social and scientific mode plays a determining role in its education. In this chapter I shall consider the ways in which the notion of utility enters into American education.

Misconstructions of Utility in Education

Within the sphere of utility in education arises the notion of its contradictory: educational inutility. (There is also another opposition; the contrary of a useful education is one that is acquired for its own sake and is in no way defined by its use. I shall reserve discussion of this kind of education for the end of the chapter.) But there is uselessness and uselessness. I shall begin with the perversions and misconstructions of utility, with abuses of education.

First and most pernicious is the perversion of the educational process into a mere formalism, an instrument of mere advancement, namely, when the chief or sole purpose is certification. There is nothing wrong with acknowledging stamina and passable work produced even against inclination. But the total and cynical setting aside of all substance for the mere externality of good grades or a diploma represents a real corruption, instituted by false teachers with the connivance of false students. Naturally, only a debased subject matter is amenable to treatment of this sort; it is utterly impossible to engage in true learning in this way. There are many explanations but no excuse for this perversion of learning. It is an indignity in education that any student should meet with open rebellion or quick departure.

Second, and most common, there is a narrow utilitarianism, a premature vocationalism. Here people too young to know themselves and too uneducated to learn easily are encouraged to acquire specific skills for immediate economic reasons. This, like the previous item, is not peculiar to American education, except for the irony of it. For whereas in planned economies such sacrifices are enforced in the name of social productiveness, here they are urged for private profit. The language of such an attitude is:

> Today we in education must recognize that it is our duty to provide our students also with salable skills. . . . To send young men and women into today's world armed only with Aristotle, Freud and Hemingway is like sending a lamb into the lion's den. . . . But if we give young men and women a useful skill, we give them not only a means to earn a good living, but also the opportunity to do something constructive and useful to society. [U.S. Education Commissioner T. H. Bell, 1974.]

This plan is tantamount to consigning the young to subservience and redundancy, for "today's world" and its economic situation are precisely what should not determine preparation. People so trained get stuck in uncongenial careers that may even cease to be economically advantageous in "tomorrow's world." Furthermore, those who lack a good grounding must learn laboriously and lengthily in schools what the well-educated acquire quickly by themselves, a chief example from experience being computer programming, a subject hard to learn in proportion to the narrowness of one's preparation. Accordingly, the very notion of "functional literacy," of teaching the young to read for mundane purposes, seems to me wrong in principle and ultimately counterproductive.

The greatest trouble is that the deprivation undergone by people so trained often does not appear until middle age. Besides, the young can expect to live longer than their parents—it seems mean to force them to add that time to their old age only; why should not some of it go to their youth?

Finally, there is a misconstruction of enlightened utility that has to do with the notion that education should make one above all useful to others, an improver of society.[5] Students themselves sometimes display a certain dubious innocence in this matter. There are some who go to college to learn how to "affect the lives of others," how to "solve the problems of society," how to "change the world," and they state these aims with the perfect certainty that they are feasible and desirable:

When I think of the lust for action which continually tickles and spurs all the millions of young Europeans who cannot bear boredom and themselves, then I apprehend that there must be in them lust for suffering in some way, in order to derive from that suffering a probable cause for doing, for a deed. Need is needful! Hence the shouting of the politicians, hence the many made-up, exaggerated "critical needs" of all possible classes and the blind readiness to believe in them. This young world demands that there should come or become visible *from the outside* not happiness—but unhappiness; and their imagination is busy even beforehand with forming it into a monster, so that they can afterwards fight with a monster. [Nietzsche, *The Gay Science*, I, 56.]

These covert forms of self-realizations come to grief, I think, both for what they preclude and for what they presume. Premature preoccupation with the problematic, with persistent malaise and impending catastrophe is no sounder for college students than for children, who are well known to be the more competent to deal with trouble the happier and stabler their upbringing. So too for students: They will deal with difficulties, indeed will formulate them, in a much more trustworthy way for having been inducted into the goods of their own civilization and for having taken time to acquire some cultivation, "to know the best that has been thought and said in the world," in Matthew Arnold's phrase. Aristotle makes a distinction of the greatest importance to the educational enterprise. He distinguishes between thinking about truths and ends and deliberating about ways and means. (*Nicomachean Ethics*, III, 1112.) My argument will be that the former is the most proper object of education, and it moreover leads to a less floundering practicality, for all these ambitions—to affect people, solve problems, change the world—require the most careful formulations of what is desirable. Nothing could be more ill-conceived than a whole curriculum based on urgent social and personal problems, like the "survival curriculum" someone has recently proposed. On the contrary, it seems to me that an education is much more likely to prepare for action in the world if it, like the Buxtehude passacaglia in Auden's poem, makes

> Our minds a *civitas* of sound
> Where nothing but assent was found
> For art had set in order sense,
> And feeling and intelligence,
> And from its ideal order grew
> Our local understanding too.
>
> ["New Year Letter," pt. I.]

Besides the harmful futility of having students take on the burdens of the world, there is also a danger of encouraging their natural propensity for self-flagellation, especially in these United States, where expansive self-criticism is endemic: "Now, all these dire self-insultings, self-mockings, at length lead to a pleasure which often attains to supreme heights of voluptuousness. Let me beg of you, gentlemen, to seize the first opportunity of listening to the groans of a cultured man of the nineteenth century who is suffering from a toothache." (Dostoevsky, *Letters from the Underworld* I, iv.) "Social problems" are, for all their reality, the toothaches of the twentieth century.

The presumption in coming to school to learn to solve human problems is that human affairs are amenable to something like an algebraic treatment, that they can be clearly formulated in terms of knowns and unknowns, and that they maybe foretold as well as resolved by an application of the proper technique. It is a faith encouraged by certain academics who, though no less mere theoreticians than any of their colleagues, want to invest their subject with irresistible urgency. Be that as it may, the mere formulation of such a problem represents, as I shall argue in the chapter on Tradition, so enormous a rational determination that students need a thorough intellectual foundation to give them some critical independence with respect to the whole genre of theories constructed for practical applications.

Educational Inutility

There are types of learning that are useless in no pejorative, or in only a mildly deprecatory, sense. They exist, usually precariously, within a world determined by utility and in opposition to it.

Among these is pure humanistic scholarship. It is certainly

affected by the notion of usefulness: It is a disciplined cumulative and corporate enterprise, held together by each scholar's professional duty to know of the opinions of all his fellow scholars, expressed in a web of references. It is progressive, at least insofar as certain concerns are superseded and drop out of sight, and, most of all, it is by obligation "productive." On the other hand, except for certain moments when such scholarship becomes incidentally serviceable, it is proudly gratuitous. The highly specialized fields of research are chosen because they are vacant or because they appeal to the scholar as scholar. But the results are not intended to be humanly very significant or much in demand, except perhaps internally, in the same scholarly community that stakes out the problems. This perennial and interlaced activity in pursuit of what Bacon calls *vermiculate questions* really is not for any particular purpose; it simply represents the corporate life of the academic world.

A more worldly but also more leisurely kind of learning is the so-called gentlemen's education, which is designed neither for scholarship nor for vocational skills. It is now practically defunct as an admitted species (though of course it continues in camouflaged versions), having been absorbed into scholarly preparation on the one hand and disintegrated before charges of elitism on the other. This "gentlemen's education" is sometimes identified with liberal education, namely, when the latter is considered as a mere embellishment essentially for the leisured classes, or when, on the other hand, a gentleman is thought of as a universally or particularly desirable type.[6] In Jefferson's day, liberal education could still be regarded as gentlemen's education in the latter sense, as a practical preparation for those who were to be charged with public office. But in the course of the last century the opposition *practical* and *liberal* comes more and more naturally. Behind it is a distinction from the realm of utility, that between *useful* and *ornamental*. It turns up in almost all the writers on education of the Enlightenment. Here is a typical passage: "As to their *Studies*, it would be well if they could be taught *every Thing* that is useful, and *every Thing* that is ornamental: But Art is long, and their Time is short. It is therefore propos'd that they learn those Things that are likely to be *most useful* and *most ornamental.*" (Franklin, "Proposals Relating to the Education of Youth.")

Ornamental learning, then, is nonuseful and stands to the useful learning somewhat in the relation of those curlicues often placed on the plinths of early engines, obligatory embellishments without much rationale. Ornamental studies mostly pertain to language: Bacon speaks of studies good "either for pleasure in meditation, ornament in speaking or aid in business." (*On Studies*, Latin version.) In particular, the classical languages, once vital necessities, are in the course of the eighteenth century increasingly regarded as mere distinguishing ornaments. As so often, Locke marks the turn of affairs: Exact Greek and Latin is for those who want a "place amongst the Learned." Latin is still "absolutely necessary to a Gentleman," but it is conversational Latin, that is, "such knowledge as he may attain without studying the Grammar of those Tongues," the cosmopolitan *lingua franca*, that he has in mind. (*Thoughts*, 164, 168.) With the adoption of modern languages as the media for exchange of information, Latin will, it follows, become unnecessary, an item of "elegant imbecility," in Newman's phrase. But as soon as that happens, the years spent on learning the classical languages become a sort of conspicuous consumption, a mark of privilege. In the nineteenth century, a partly covert, partly open, battle against the classical curriculum is carried on in the name of democracy and utility together,[7] a battle initiated by some of the early republican writers, notably by Noah Webster, who makes all of liberal education share the stigma of making mere gentlemen: "Indeed it appears to me that what is now called a *liberal education* disqualifies a man for business."[8] In the long run, the outcome is that "both 'cultural' and 'utilitarian' subjects exist in an inorganic composite where the former are not by dominant purpose socially serviceable and the latter not liberative of imagination or thinking power. . . . The outcome of the mixture is perhaps less satisfactory than if either principle were adhered to in its purity." (Dewey, *Democracy and Education*, ch. 19.) It is, I think, an index of a deep and perennial requirement of American life (which will be defined later) that such amalgams, debased as they are, appear to be ineradicable—that the principle of utility never triumphs "in its purity."

I should mention that the chief province of ornamental learning is the so-called female accomplishments—music, drawing, dancing, playing an instrument. The latter is decried on utilitarian grounds by Rush in his treatise on the specifically American education of women, and by Webster also: "No man ever marries a woman for her performance on a harpsichord or her figure in a minuet."[9] Jefferson, however, notes that "the taste of this country, too, calls for this accomplishment more strongly" than for the others and recommends it for women as invaluable among the "ornaments . . . and the amusements of life"—but how weak an endorsement for so passionate a musician as he was! (To Burwell, 14 March 1818.)[10]

Indeed, the ornamental role to which music is consigned in the utilitarian context, and, for that matter, poetry as well, is of deep interest to all education. Locke, as usual plainest, inveighs against both; as for poetry, "Methinks the Parents should labour to have it stifled, and suppressed, as much as may be: And I know not what Reason a Father can have, to wish his Son a Poet." (*Thoughts*, 174.)[11] Fordyce goes right to the heart of the reason for the absence of fancy and fable in modern teaching; it is because we have no time: "Truth must be cast out like an heap of Pearls before us." (*Dialogues*, I, xi.) As for music, Locke says: "And I have, among Men of Parts and Business, so seldom heard anyone commended, or esteemed for having an Excellency in *Musick*, that amongst all those things, that ever came into the List of Accomplishments, I think I may give it the last place." (*Thoughts*, 197.)

I cite these passages to compare the meager standing of music in modern education with the central position as the most effective instrument of human formation assigned to it by ancient authors. The whole second book of Plato's *Laws* and the final existing chapters of Aristotle's *Politics* are devoted to the use of music in political education: "Music can provide a certain moral set of the soul, and if it can do this, it is clear that the young must be brought to it and educated in it." (*Politics* VIII, 1340b.) In particular, music has the power to make children pleased and pained in conformity with the law, to produce harmony and agreement with the polity in the least burdensome way. (*Laws* 659 d.) To be sure, for Milton some of the old power still remains. For boys, after "wrastling," music is indicated:

> The interim of unsweating themselves regularly ... may ... with profit and delight be taken up in recreating and composing their travail'd spirits with the solemn and divine harmonies of Musick heard or learnt; either while the skilful *Organist* plies his grave and fancied descant, in lofty Fugues, or the whole Symphony with artful and unimaginable touches adorn and grace the well studied chords of some choice Composer;... which if wise men and Prophets be not extreamly out, have a great power over dispositions and manners, to smooth and make them gentle from rustick harshness and distemper'd passions. [*Of Education.*]

But for its full standing as a statesman's tool it is necessary to go to the ancients. The depreciation of music is both a cause and a sign of the difficulty modern education has with the formation of civic sentiment.

USEFUL EDUCATION

I come now to true utility in education. It has three aspects: learning undertaken for use in further learning, education regarded as primarily profitable to oneself, education intended to fit one to serve others. Each of these has its own perplexities.

Ancillary Learning

Almost any learning can be useful to further learning, and some learning would scarcely be done for any other reason—for example, the inflectional paradigms that sooner or later must be committed to memory in learning a foreign language and the rules of algebraic operations. It is the mark of a good teacher to extract the intrinsic interest of even such instrumental knowledge, to allow the end to illuminate the means or, best of all, to show how the technique in fact shapes the matter to which it is applied. For example, those very dreary algebraic operations indeed assume a radical reinterpretation of our natural understanding of numbers, and something of this momentous intellectual revolution can be conveyed even to beginners. And as learning can be in the service of higher learning, so theory can come down to earth to serve in application or cross as a technique into other disciplines. The world of learning is a network of mutual utilities.

The perennial difficulty with the potentially instrumental character of almost all learning is that it taints the spirit in which learning is done. No subject is so inherently capable of being instrumental as mathematics; nowhere else are vigorous efficacy and dreary operationalism so much each other's obverse, so that beauty is forfeited to blind efficiency:

> The mathematical process in the symbolical [i.e., algebraic] method is like running a railroad through a tunneled mountain; that in the ostensive [i.e., diagrammatic] like crossing the mountain on foot. The former carries us, by a short and easy transit, to our destined point, but in miasma, darkness and torpidity; whereas the latter allows us to reach it only after time and trouble, but feasting us at each turn with glances of the earth and the heavens. [Sir William Hamilton.][12]

The paradox of instrumental learning—power wrecks pleasure—is a most serious problem of modern pedagogy that can be resolved, I will argue, only by making frequent returns to the intellectual presuppositions of such learning. The danger to the Republic is that the more potent such learning becomes, the fewer people elect it, for as it becomes more sophisticated it becomes less accessible. It is a sad fact that, in the displacement of language by mathematical science that characterizes modernity, science has not gained what language has lost—the adherence of the whole educated community.

Individual Utility

Frankly and hardheadedly useful training has been an educational preoccupation of this Republic from its inception. Early republican college charters regularly made *usefulness and reputation* the educational aim. The early educational writers, spontaneous as well as studied Lockeans, all declared for a utility, albeit one not incompatible with liberal learning. Over a century later, precisely the same efforts were made at "introducing into our educational system the aim of utility, to take its place in dignity by the side of culture, and to connect education with life by making it purposeful and useful." ("Report of the Commission on National and Vocational Education," 1914.)[13] More than another half-century later, the same call is still being issued. (I shall have occasion throughout this inquiry to attempt a defense of the extraordinary tenacity displayed by non-utilitarian education in the face of these long-standing demands.)

The two poles of utilitarian education are implicit in the ambiguous phrase, "a useful and productive member of society." I think the usual implication is that in doing well for oneself one is helping others. At least in this Republic it is the prevailing view that the public realm is to be served by private success. In other societies, utility does not have this double sense: "In the center of education the Party places the development of a Communist attitude of all members of society toward work. Work for the good of society is everyone's sacred duty." ("Program of the Communist Party of the Soviet Union.")[14] Naturally, some special educational dilemmas arise from the American notion that private and public utility are ordinarily coincident.

The bluntest object of utilitarian schooling is to make a living, to make money, that is, to produce means. The essential perverseness of this end has been exposed from Plato (*Republic* I, 346) to Marx ("Estranged Labor");[15] obviously, the essence of no craft (except investment) is moneymaking; obviously, labor that is "merely a means to needs external to it" is mortifying. But as things are constituted, parents are naturally anxious about the livelihood of their children (who, when not tampered with, most often have a sort of glorious indifference to it). Hence it is the obligation of an educational institution, not indeed to meet this concern, but to be crystal clear about the relation of its program to making a living—whether that relation is direct or remote or nonexistent. In particular, there is a very ancient doubt about the economic usefulness of reflective inquiry, expressed in the story of Thales, the first of the nature philosophers. He was taunted for his philosopher's poverty, and having, by means of his physical speculations, predicted a heavy olive harvest, by an application of practical wisdom made down payments on all the local olive presses and thence a fortune (Aristotle, *Politics* I, 1259a.) Most colleges purvey some implausibly updated version of this tale, but it seems to me that they would do better to state forthrightly that true education, without in the least despising it, has only an inessential relation to moneymaking.

Next under the heading of individual utility, at least in this country, is the achievement of competence, that is, vocational or professional training: "If education is preparation for life, and if practically everyone's life and opportunities for self-expression and self-fulfillment include work, then only the successfully employable are successfully educated. . . . Culture and vocation are inseparable and unseverable aspects of humanity." (Advisory Council on Vocational Education, 1968.)[16] Training for self-fulfillment through a *calling*, a vocation (the term is not taken from religious life accidentally) is the learning most devotedly advocated of any in America. It is thought of as a welcome democratizing influence, as giving scope to a variety of utilities, as exerting a healthy influence on general education by making it less bookish. (Commission on National Aid to Education, 1914.)[17] Almost everyone, including academics— who are, after all, themselves consumers of goods and services— agrees that any training that increases competence should be given support and dignity, provided the institutionalization of manual training does not inhibit the American jack-of-all-trades style that brings so many people in this country so near to Marx's postrevolutionary man, able "to hunt in the morning, fish in the afternoon, rear cattle in the evening, criticize after dinner, . . . without ever becoming hunter, fisherman, shepherd or critic." (*The German Ideology*, "Feuerbach," 1a.) A difficulty arises only in the perennial attempt of educational writers to argue that liberal and vocational training are convertible. To be sure, they are naturally compatible—but they are emphatically not coincident, as I shall argue in the last section of this chapter, "The Search for Ends," and both are better served by crisp delimitations.[18]

As the ultimate form of individual educational utility, I would list all kinds of self-formation: the acquisitions of refined skills and the cultivation of taste and judgment. I have in mind what is meant by the German word *Bildung*, a kind of shaping up, a sharpening of the discriminating arts and powers, particularly with respect to human matters. It can be regarded as utilitarian because it is often not itself a very pleasant process, although a means to enjoyment and security. Under this heading comes William James's definition of higher education as that which "should enable us to *know a good man when we see him,*" as well as the inverse case suggested by an English novelist thus: "To dislike her was the sign of a liberal education."[19]

Social Education

In the early Republic the question of citizen education, of forming the young to become "useful instruments for the public," as Jefferson put it in his "Bill for the Diffusion of Knowledge," was ultimately paramount. To be sure, the terms of the problem have shifted: from breeding political responsibility to engendering a feeling for social justice, from preserving a passion for liberty to inducing sensitivity for equal rights, from the devising a proper preparation for public affairs to the concern with abolition of educational inequalities. But I would argue that, in spite of the slippage of terms, certain fundamental preoccupations of republican education and their attendant dilemmas are perennial, while with respect to the more current terms, the Founders' views can almost be said to represent a fresh new approach.

Before setting out these views, I want to make a point about the relation of such educational purposes to their realization, which cannot help but be quite different in different polities. To frame the argument, let me use extreme cases.

There is, on one end, that polity constructed in thought, a pattern "laid up in heaven," Plato's *Republic* (IX, 592b). It is not a plan intended for realization but an inquiry into the relation of philosophical theory to political practice. Socrates allows himself a radical revision of natural human relations for the guardians of the polity: To achieve a perfectly unified community of pain and pleasure, all particularizing blood and sexual relations are abolished in favor of a communization of marriage partners and children (V, 462); the guardianship of the polity is in the hands of those found by a presumably feasible test to be fitted by nature for the education devised by the founders (VII); the rest of the citizens live under no particular discipline at all. What characterizes this governors' upbringing is that it leads out of, rather than into, the political arena. It is a philosophical education that initiates the participants into a transpolitical wisdom, a view of being in its wholeness, "the Good." The philosopher kings are abruptly projected into their offices—practical wisdom, not political theory, mediates between philosophical contemplation and practical politics. The inevitable degeneration of the community is the consequence of the irrationality of breeding—the educational scheme is not at fault.

A diametric opposite is the realized modern totalitarian state. By a totalitarian state I mean one in which in principle no facet of life is left untouched by the prevailing ideology. An ideology is a rational theory that is no longer in the state of inquiry; it is rather an accepted teaching to which the totality of actions and opinions is expected to conform, a theory "intended to change the world, not interpret it":

> Under the conditions of socialism and the building of Communist society, where spontaneous economic development has given way to a conscious organization of production and of the total life of society, and theory is translated into practice day by day, the formation of a scientific world-view of the workers of Soviet society on the basis of Marxism-Leninism as a self-sufficient and harmonious system of philosophical, economic, social and political views, gains primary significance. ["The Tasks of the Party in the Area of Ideology, Training, Education, Science and Culture," "Program of the Communist Party of the Soviet Union," 1961.][20]

Here, not the privacies of human relations but the spontaneities of the economic system are the targets of the founding revolution. The guardianship is in the hands, not of the followers of a philosophical way, but of the members of a political party. The training of the members of society is through the ruling ideology, which is a "scientific" practical social theory. The slippage between principles and practices will evidently be considerable. The causes are numerous: ideological factionalism, bureaucratic inefficiency, ineradicable residues of tradition, the inevitably reasserted pragmatism of any stable society, and, above all, the insuperable fact that the actual matter taught in the educational system comes from an older intellectual tradition not immediately amenable to the ideology.

American education lies between the extremes of ideality and reality, philosophy and ideology, community and conformity, family and economic system. Therefore, the answer to the question, "How ought a citizen education to fit into the polity?", which is to some degree manifest in other polities, is full of oppositions in this Republic: tradition-revolution, school-life, private-public schooling, excellence-equality, citizen-statesman, citizen-philosopher. Let me now consider these in the light of early republican views on the relation of education to social usefulness.

Tradition-Revolution. I begin with the first part of the preamble of Jefferson's "Bill for the More General Diffusion of Knowledge" (1779), which was never adopted by the legislature and never forgotten by him.

> Whereas it appeareth that however certain forms of government are better calculated than others to protect individuals in the free exercise of their natural rights, and are at the same time themselves better guarded against degeneracy, yet experience hath shewn, that even under the best forms, those entrusted with power have, in time, and by slow operations, perverted it into tyranny; and it is believed that the most effectual means of preventing this would be, to illuminate, as far as practicable, the minds of the people at large, and more especially to give them knowledge of those facts, which history exhibiteth, that, possessed thereby of the experience of other ages and countries, they may be enabled to know ambition under all its shapes, and prompt to exert their natural powers to defeat its purposes; And whereas it is

generally true that the people will be happiest whose laws are best, and are best administered, and that laws will be wisely formed, and honestly administered, in proportion as those who form and administer them are wise and honest. . . .

There follows a comprehensive system of public education, including both institutions and curriculum. The preamble is a remarkable statement of educational aims. In the midst of a revolution it asserts that the best of governments, presumably even the republic about to be established, will degenerate, and that the paramount object of education is to make the people prompt to defeat the purposes of political ambition, that is, to make them perpetually ready for revolution. Furthermore, it claims that ultimately even a government of laws is a government of men, and it omits any reference to the power of the laws themselves to form citizens. It is indeed a thoroughly Jeffersonian statement—fully in accordance with his distrust of a settled polity and his therapeutic view of revolution. "I hold that a little rebellion now and then is a good thing, and as necessary in the political world as storms in the physical." (To Madison, 30 January 1787.) The radically suspicious, rebelliously critical element that surfaced in American education in the sixties had a certain right to call on Jefferson—not, however, insofar as it was opposed to study, particularly of the past. It was precisely historical studies that Jefferson regarded as the preparation for responsible resistance.

In certain respects opposed to this education for revolution was the effort of the early republican writers to turn education toward the formation not only of a specifically American character but also of a stable republican type. In the interest of the former they, Jefferson included, oppose the European education of very young Americans. The "objects of an useful American education," that is, "Classical knowledge, modern languages, chiefly French, Spanish, and Italian; mathematics, natural philosophy, natural history, civil history, and ethics," are to be gotten quite well in America. In Europe a young student conceives an abhorrence for "the lovely equality which the poor enjoy with the rich" and other antirepublican sentiments. (To Bannister, 15 October 1785, from Paris.) Webster, particularly, agrees: It is sometimes advisable to complete a course of study abroad, but never to go too early or to continue there too long. Indigenous education, Dr. Rush asserts, is necessary both to make the population more homogeneous and to shape patriots for the new country: "The principle of patriotism stands in need of the reinforcement of *prejudice*, and it is well known that our strongest prejudices in favour of our country are formed in the first one and twenty years of our lives." But most of all, the object of education is to shape citizens of a republic. Dr. Rush puts it rather repulsively in this same essay, entitled "Thoughts upon the Mode of Education proper in a Republic": "I consider it as possible to convert men into republican machines." He means only citizens who perform properly their part in "the great machine of the government,"—in those days a machine was still a benignly efficient instrument. He recommends a thorough initiation into the workings of republican institutions, the kind of course we used to call *civics*. It is a curricular idea effectively proposed later for the common school system by Horace Mann.[21] But most important to Rush is training in republican virtue—he is the most antique of all the writers in his conceptions; accordingly, he (as Mann would later) recommends recourse to music, specifically, to singing, for forming civic sentiment.

That brings me to the two great difficulties associated with this opposition, tradition -revolution. The first of these has to do precisely with the education of national republican sentiment, the second with the very notion of the formation of a republican patriot, not to say a machine.

I have already referred to the depreciation in the modern utilitarian republic of music in the large antique sense, in which it includes all the Muses' patronage, such as poetry and dancing. An attempt to give the context of this eclipse of the imagination is reserved for my last chapter, on Rationality. The implication of importance here is that the generation of patriotic passion becomes a real problem in a congenitally sober polity, whose pride is peaceful prosperity privately enjoyed. Such a society has no natural bent toward communal life. As Tocqueville put it, "Democracy loosens social ties, but tightens natural ones; it brings kindred more closely together, while it throws citizens apart." (*Democracy in America* II, bk. 3, viii.)

It is a cause as well as a consequence of this bias toward privacy that the public realm arouses the interested feelings more than the affections or the esthetic sense. Whether utility can at all appear beautiful was a serious question to the generation of the Founding Fathers. A man of such vibrant sobriety as Alexander Hamilton could indeed find a disinterested sort of delight in the vast liveliness of a working business community: "There is something noble and magnificent in the perspective of a great Foederal Republic, closely linked in the pursuit of a common interest, tranquil and prosperous at home, respectable abroad."[22] But whether these mundane blessings, which induce what Tocqueville calls a "patriotism of reflection" rather than of feeling, can capture the imagination of the young is another matter, particularly since it is perfectly natural to this Republic that its patriotic manifestations should tend toward philistinism. The long-range effect has been the discrediting of patriotism and a movement toward those centrifugal loyalties—"ethnic" in our day—which these writers wanted to weaken by building a national character through a patriotic education. The simple fact is that the noble exhilaration of the unique Revolution and the Founding, by the very reason of their success, were displaced by the secure comfort of a continuing Republic.[23]

This aspect of the Founding paradox was much on Lincoln's mind. It demands not so much a revolutionary tradition as the converse, the assumption of the Revolution into the tradition. In his speech, "The Perpetuation of Our Political Institutions," he proposes its resolution: It is a replacement of the romantic revolutionary passion centered on the Declaration by a passionately rational reverence centered on the Constitution, a second Founding to be perpetually reenacted. Lincoln not only argues but exemplifies the possibility that there might be poetry in the public realm.

The second aspect of the founding paradox concerns the question of republican dogma itself. To train serviceable republicans is, after all, as Rush so ingenuously puts it, to instill a prejudice. All the writers agree that it is to be a peculiar prejudice, a prejudice in favor of liberty. The young are to be trained to resist tyranny. Now, the paradox in thought of this compulsion to freedom is patent, and its real consequences were immediate. It appeared in the one notoriously dubious aspect of Jefferson's founding of his university, his view that "it is certainly very material that the true doctrines of liberty, as exemplified in our Political System, should be inculcated in those who are to sustain and may administer it." (To Madison, 8 February 1825.) He proceeded to realize this opinion by instituting as the "norma docendi" certain textbooks concerned not only with politics (which is often pointed out) but also with what he regarded as its proper philosophical basis (which is rarely remarked).[24] The trouble is that the short list of political texts— Locke's *Second Essay on Government*, Sidney's *Discourses on Government*, the Declaration, the *Federalist*, the Virginia Resolutions on the Alien and Sedition Laws, Washington's Valedictory Address—which, except perhaps for the fifth item, appear innocently standard now, was constructed in a spirit of guarding against the danger of "rank Federalists" and their "unsound opinions." In other words, it was not only republican but Republican; factionalism had intruded—an ever-present but not totally unavoidable danger in political education. It is, after all, also possible to construct a balanced reading list of fundamentally republican texts, to keep the founding issues alive. The philosophical issue will be addressed in the chapters on Tradition and Rationality.

By the end of the century after the Founding, the development of a specifically American democratic social character, already evident to Tocqueville in 1831, had on its own proceeded far enough for schooling to assume a wider mandate than the Founders had ever conceived or could ever have approved: "The social relation of a child is frequently taken in too limited a sense, as when training to citizenship in the narrow sense is in mind.... Apart from the thought of participation in social life the school has no end nor aim." (Dewey, *Ethical Principles Underlying Education*, Thesis 3.) Hence, the republican citizen, resistant to tyranny and bent on self-improvement, turns into the socially adjusted individual willing to conform; political education is expanded to social training; the pedagogue assumes the role of an unelected legislator. But in reaction, the problem of the individual and his self-expression eventually comes to the fore; discipline and standards are relaxed. This complex of educational dilemmas is familiar enough. I am suggesting that a recovery of the deep and vital founding paradoxes will prove therapeutic.

School-Life. The question whether educational institutions should be isolated from, or extensions of, "life," is of great importance in the pedagogy of a republic. One extreme is the ivory tower: "I have had sight of the perfect place of learning in my thought: a free place and a various . . . itself a little world . . . calm Science seated there, recluse, ascetic like a nun . . . like the world in having all men's life at heart . . . but unlike the world in its self-possession." (Woodrow Wilson, 1896.)[25] On the other, then, is the demand (which came to a head in the sixties) for a thorough politicization, for direct interventions by educational institutions into political and social issues, a demand that was a foreseeable consequence of the prior use of the universities as social problem-solving agencies.

And beyond either of these views, there is the appeal to schools to dissolve themselves in favor of life; students "should not *play* life, or *study* it merely, while the community supports them at this expensive game, but earnestly *live* it from beginning to end. How could youths better learn to live than by at once trying the experiment of living? Methinks this would exercise their minds as much as mathematics." (Thoreau, *Walden; or Life in the Woods*, ch. 1.) The converse possibility is also urged: "to make each one of our schools an embryonic community life, active with types of occupations that reflect the life of the larger society." (Dewey, *The School and Society*, ch. 1.)

Another issue, furthermore, cuts across the distinction of school and life, that of book learning and original reflection: "Meek young men grow up in libraries, believing it their duty to accept the views which Cicero, which Locke, which Bacon, have given; forgetful that Cicero, Locke, and Bacon were only young men in libraries when they wrote these books. Hence instead of Man thinking, we have the bookworm." (Emerson, *The American Scholar*.)

Similarly, a pleasure in books is sometimes regarded as detrimental to business, which "is in some sense mechanical":[26] "Indeed it appears to me that what is now called a liberal education disqualifies a man for business." (Webster.) Webster recommends only enough academic education to leave time for an apprenticeship before the age of twenty-one. However, he is somewhat unusual in holding this opinion. By and large, the early writers have an unclouded faith in formal learning. Well they might, for the Revolution itself had just been carried off by men whose intellectual vigor was such that their application of book learning to programs of action was immediate and continuous.[27] Accordingly, Jefferson writes:

> Education ... engrafts a new man on the native stock, and improves what in his nature was vicious and perverse into qualities of virtue and social worth. And it cannot be but that each generation succeeding to the knowledge acquired by all those who preceded it, adding to it their own acquisitions and discoveries, and handing the mass down for successive and constant accumulation, must advance the knowledge and well-being of mankind ... to a time which no one can fix and foresee. [Jefferson, "Rockfish Gap Report."]

This faith stems partly from the fact that in the spirit of the Enlightenment the Founders expected that an appropriate theory could be developed for *any* practical undertaking. For example, Rush asks that the principles of commerce and money be "reduced to such a system as to be intelligible and agreeable to a young man"; in other words, he wants business courses. At Jefferson's university, "All the branches of science deemed useful at this day, shall be taught in their highest degree." (To Ticknor, 25 November 1817.) The value of such schooling is an early republican axiom. There is no hint of the romantic reaction, the surfeit and disenchantment, that this eager and eventually bloated course-making and -taking engenders in the long run. Those for whom universally accessible education was "an Utopian dream" (Jefferson to Correa de Serra, 25 November 1817) would naturally not foresee the dangers of modern academia.

In general, the early writers were untroubled either by the vital ancient distinction between the theoretical and the practical life or by the unhappy modern division between academic life and "Life." They knew well the problem of making school more practical, but it never occurred to them that it ought to be made more lifelike (with the result of wrecking the crisp distinction between book study and leisure, without in the least aiding the application of learning to life in the real, unsupervised world). They were still innocent of the peculiar degeneration and devaluation education undergoes when it is compulsory or easily accessible, or of the dangers that face large, powerful universities involved with business and government through applied research. It never occurred to them that there might be a demand for confounding the preparation for affairs with their mature transaction, or for the corporate intervention of institutions of learning in political questions,[28] or, on the contrary, for the isolation and purity of the academy. Not that some version of the rudiments of these perplexities was not present in the post-Revolutionary schools. Rather, like most enthusiastic planners, they foresaw much, but not the problematic consequences of their success. In respect to this particular issue, however, their use to us is not so much in furnishing the root terms of a difficulty as in providing the example of a healthy frame of mind. Some of the vitality is returned to study if teachers simply display some trust in it. Further aspects of this problem will be taken up in the chapter on Tradition.

Public-Private Education. In the original terms of the debate, this opposition was pedagogical in the largest sense: Should children attend school in common under public supervision or receive private tutoring? In other words: Should education be institutionalized? The influential ancient writers are all for public education: "Since the purpose of the whole city is one, it is clear that education, too, is of necessity one and the same for all, and its care should be public and not private. For the way it is now, everyone takes care of his children in private and teaches them whatever private learning he thinks right. But public matters ought to be pursued in public." (Aristotle. *Politics* VIII 1337 a.) Quintilian, too, although admitting the arguments against common education, namely, corruption of morals and individual neglect, favors common education so as to accustom the future man of affairs to living in the full light of the public realm (*res publica*) and to have the benefit of the variety and competition of a school (I, ii). Here Bacon sides with the ancients. (*De Augmentis Scientiarum*, IV, 4.) But three of the most indicative moderns, Montaigne, Locke, and Rousseau resolutely oppose school attendance, which exposes the child to "malapertness, tricking, or violence." (Locke, *Thoughts*, 70.) The cause of Locke's resistance is that he considers the first aim of education to be character training, the instilling of virtue. "Vertue is harder to be got, than a Knowledge of the World," where virtue, "the most necessary of those Endowments, that belong to a Man or a Gentleman" (70, 135) means a kind of sturdy ingenuousness. The understanding that the true breeding ground of character is the family is very much an element in American schooling.

The early republican writers regard Locke's views as a real stumbling block, but they nonetheless argue for public education, sometimes citing Quintilian and other ancients: Common learning supplies the benefits of healthy emulation, classroom concentration, independent reflection, diversity of association, better apparatus, and the forming of friendships. The last of these is of special importance in a republican education. The poet of the Revolution, Joel Barlow, wrote in praise of liberal education that "The liberal sciences are in their nature republican; they delight in reciprocal communication; they cherish fraternal feelings, and lead to a freedom of intercourse, combined with the restraint of society, which contribute together to our improvement."[29] The passage, to be sure, refers to higher education, but a similar benefit is valued in the lower schools—there is, again, something antique in this understanding that "friendship seems to hold political communities together." (Aristotle *Nicomachean Ethics* VIII, 1155a.) While this view of the political bond of city states is too intimate for the cool-headed Founders of a great republic to espouse as doctrine, it certainly had its place in their private relations, for example, in Jefferson's friendship with Madison and, in old age, with

Adams. Indeed, they welcomed public schooling as an agency for inducing the *fraternity* whose absence as a political watchword so significantly distinguishes the American from the French Revolution.

The early writers (Rush, Webster, Coram, Smith, Knox, and, of course, Jefferson) concluded from these advantages of common education that there should be a compulsory, publicly financed, and locally supervised nonsectarian school system. Those are the very notions comprised in the modern meaning of *public education*.[30] *Private*, then, means, on the contrary, attended by choice, privately financed, and free in planning a curriculum, including religious instruction. (For Mann, the opposite of *public* was now *parochial* schooling.) In secondary schools all of these items would of course be strictly limited by the public authorities.

With respect to the colleges, my main concern, there were no strictly private schools in this country in the early days. The colonial colleges were financed from both public and private sources; sectarian and secular influences were thoroughly entangled with each other. Even in post-Revolutionary times the private colleges usually received state money; exclusively private financing began only after the Civil War, when the state universities had drawn all the public funds to themselves.[31]

The immediate reason for the burgeoning of private colleges after the Revolution was the response to the Constitutional nonsectarianism of the public realm as well as a reaction to the antireligious coloration of the Founders. But the long-range issue was the question of the control of educational institutions. The crucial event, which assured the unique dual system characteristic of the United States, was Chief Justice Marshall's *Dartmouth College Opinion* of 1819. The New Hampshire legislature had attempted to convert the college into a public institution. The case was argued by Daniel Webster, whose peroration dwelled on the vulnerability of small private institutions: "It is, Sir, as I have said, a small College. And yet, *there are those who love it.*" Marshall decided against the state: "Does every teacher of youth become a public officer, and do donations for the purpose of education necessarily become public property?" No.

The will of the state could not be substituted for that of the private donors, for such a donation constitutes a contract respecting private property that no state legislature can impair. The integrity of small independent institutions, and so the possibility of a vigorous educational pluralism, was henceforth protected, at least from encroachment by the state. The other danger, perennial and now crucial, is, of course, financial.

The early republican writers, on the other hand, were advocates of a state and even a national system of higher education, one and all: Rush, Webster, Smith, Lafitte du Courteil, Knox, Barlow, and, above all, du Pont de Nemours, who in 1800 wrote an original sketch on national education in response to a request from the presidential candidate, Jefferson. In fact, each of the first six presidents proposed a national university to the Congress, all unsuccessfully.[32] They expected such centralization to make for more intellectually powerful, selectively accessible, nationally unifying institutions of learning, but they were oddly blithe about the dangers of domination such institutions exercise at their best and the mediocrity they spread at their worst. I think that it is a good guess that, had they seen a contemporary state university, they would have been very satisfied in principle but somewhat appalled at some of the actual practice. It seems to me a blessing that their enthusiasm for accessible higher education prevailed, and a blessing that it prevailed slowly enough and piecemeal enough to preserve the dualism and the pluralism of American education. Indeed, this system of public and private education is the necessary condition for the occasional generating of a type of institution that is the salt of the educational world: a school that can become exemplary through its essential institutional integrity and intensity.—*Intensity*, it seems to me, is both a less invidious and a far more telling term in education than *excellence*.

Excellence-Equality. The current discussion in education centers on the question of *equal educational opportunity*.[33] The pejorative obverse term is *elitism*. It seems to me that much depends on fixing its meaning and restricting its use. Now, when it is used of educational endeavors that are simply small or intimate or selective or special, that is, I think, a false use—the term might then as well be applied to lovemaking. But when it means *exclusionary*, selective not through self-selection or criteria of adequacy, but through a mere wish to exclude or make invidious distinctions, then some term of disapproval is in order, and it might as well be *elitism*. The confusion concerning this term seems to me to be very harmful, because it taints a principle that is necessary to educational planning: that the standard need not be the general, or the exemplary the universal. That is to say, there might be educational institutions and plans that are not large or widespread and yet represent one of the ways things ought to be.

Now unhappily, the term *excellence* is often felt to be associated with elitism; excellence and equality are felt to be incompatible. There is some real reason for that. To *excel* means literally to *rise above*, to be outstanding. One of the dilemmas facing democratic education originates in the human question whether the very good are always the very few, or whether the best and the brightest might also be the many. It is a question that aristocracies answer in principle: The best are the few. But democracies circumvent the answer by valuing fundamentally not human excellence but humanity simply. The question of excellence is left to work itself out as leisure and opportunity for learning become more universal. The hypothesis, derived from the founding axiom that all men are created equal, is that all the young have respectable abilities of various sorts. For this setting, merit is the more tolerable the less it is associated with arrogance and exclusiveness (no great loss, since genuine excellence has nothing to do with these, in any case).

The early republican writers are not, by and large, much preoccupied with the problem of intellectual excellence in education. To them it is an obvious and noninvidious fact that there will be a few children of "superior genius," that these must be given access to the highest grades of education and that from among them will come the legislators. To be sure, Jefferson especially is much concerned to "accept no mediocrity" on the faculty of his university. (To Correa de Serra, 25 November 1817.) But this concern, like that of all the other writers, is with finding rather than accommodating excellence. They are much more interested in the enlightenment of citizens and the diffusion of knowledge to them. They all regard this enterprise with that optimism which the notion of a universal public system of education indeed requires.

But what occupies them most urgently is the education of citizens to *virtue*: "The *virtues* of men are of more consequence to society than their *abilities*, and for this reason the *heart* should be cultivated with more assiduity than the *head*." (Webster.) Now virtue has an antique ring to it. Indeed, it is the rendering of a Roman term and ultimately of the Greek term *aretē*. It means an excellence (and is indeed sometimes translated as *excellence*), a superior power either to accomplish something or to govern oneself. It is in the latter sense that Montesquieu considers virtue the unique requirement of republics. For that reason,

> It is in a republican government that the whole power of education is required.... [For] virtue is a self-renunciation, which is ever arduous and painful.
> This virtue may be defined as the love of the laws and of our country. As such love requires a constant preference of public to private interest, it is the source of all private virtues....
> Everything, therefore, depends on establishing this love in a republic; and to inspire it ought to be the principal business of education. [*Spirit of the Laws* I, iv, 5.]

Montesquieu's republic is a small, close-knit, directly governed city state, not a large, heterogeneous, modern federation. (Jefferson is critical of Montesquieu precisely on that score—for not understanding the modern principle of representation; Jefferson's love of the laws, too, has strict limits.)[34] In a modern commercial republic the character of virtue is altered to accommodate the notion of the coincidence of private and public utility:

> I doubt whether men were more virtuous in aristocratic ages than in others, but they were incessantly talking of the beauties of virtue, and its utility was only studied in secret. But since ... every man's thoughts are centered in himself,

moralists are alarmed by this idea of self-sacrifice and they no longer venture to present it to the human mind. They therefore content themselves with inquiring whether the personal advantage of each member of the community does not consist in working for the good of all. . . . And it is held as a truth that man serves himself in serving his fellow creatures and that his private interest is to do good. [Tocqueville, *Democracy in America* II, bk. 2, viii.]

Evidently, from a truly modern vantage point Montesquieu's virtue looks aristocratic.

The virtue the early writers wish to inculcate is a mean between the grand, selfless passion of ancient republics and the calculatingly enlightened self-interest of modern moralists. They wish to "meliorate the heart," to instill "sensibility" (something like our "sensitivity"), to foster "universal philanthropy." It is the sociable virtue referred to above, a benevolent utilitarianism.[35] For when Jefferson says that "nature has constituted *utility* to man, the standard and test of virtue" (To Law, 13 July 1814), he goes on to make it clear that the utility is to others— the opposite of *virtuous* is *injurious*. The Founding writers, whose orthodoxy is otherwise somewhat feeble, even enlist Christianity in behalf of this modern republican virtue: "A Christian . . . cannot fail of being a republican, for every precept of the Gospel inculcates those degrees of humility, self-denial, and brotherly kindness which are directly opposed to the pride of monarchy." (Rush.)[36]

Again, specifically political virtue is, at least for Jefferson, something modest and unimperious: It is honesty, the quality of not lying, cheating, or stealing. In his youth he had instructed the British king that "the whole art of government consists in the art of being honest." (*A Summary View of the Rights of British America*.) In his "Bill for the General Diffusion of Knowledge" he used the terms *wise and honest* parallel to *genius and virtue*, and he makes the vice opposite to *Justice*, *Deceit*. (To Short, 31 October 1819.)

With respect to the moral virtues, these writers, then, conceive of a humane and honest citizenry, informed with a social virtue too negative and universal to be called excellence. With respect to intellectual virtue, on the other hand, sharp differences in individual capacities as well as a firmly fixed distinction between the uneducated and the educated are taken as given. But just because these are natural distinctions,

> it becomes expedient for promoting the publick happiness that those persons, whom nature hath endowed with genius and virtue, should be rendered by liberal education worthy to receive, and able to guard the sacred deposit of the rights and liberties of their fellow citizens, and that they should be called to that charge without regard to wealth, birth or other accidental condition or circumstance; but the indigence of the greater number disabling them from so educating, at their own expence, those of their children whom nature hath fitly formed and disposed to become useful instruments for the public, it is better that such should be sought for and educated at the common expence of all, than that the happiness of all should be confided to the weak or wicked. [Second part of Preamble, "Bill for the Diffusion of Knowledge."]

Similarly, since "the mass of our citizens may be divided into two classes—the laboring and the learned," it is of particular importance that the laborers should have a solid elementary education "to qualify them for their pursuits and duties." (To Carr, 7 September 1814.)

Jefferson, at least, expects a university education to render its beneficiaries "examples of virtue to others." ("Rockfish Gap Report.") This hope suggests the incipient paradox of intellectual excellence and moral equality: Can a "meritocracy" (for that is what most of the writers, including Jefferson, contemplated) ever be exemplary in a mildly and humanly negative republican virtue? And, conversely, will a citizenry conscious of its equal moral worth tolerate such excellence?

Citizen-Statesman. For Jefferson, as indeed for the other writers, it is obvious that the future officers of this Republic should have a preparation similar to that required for the learned professions, Without meaning to make any invidious distinctions in respect to republican equality, they consider it a matter of course that the "mass of citizens" will not obtain such a higher education.

So much the more does this difference make a solid universal primary education a republican necessity.

The preeminent text for comparing the character of the two educations is Jefferson's "Rockfish Gap Report" of 1818, the founding document of the University of Virginia:

> The objects of this primary education determine its character and limits. These objects would be,
>
> [1.] To give to every citizen the information he needs for the transaction of his own business;
>
> [2.] To enable him to calculate for himself, and to express and preserve his ideas, his contracts and accounts, in writing;
>
> [3.] To improve, by reading, his morals and faculties;
>
> [4.] To understand his duties to his neighbors and country, and to discharge with competence the functions confided to him by either;
>
> [5.] To know his rights; to exercise with order and justice those he retains; to choose with discretion the fiduciary of those he delegates; and to notice their conduct with diligence, with candor, and judgment;
>
> [6.] And, in general, to observe with intelligence and faithfulness all the social relations under which he shall be placed.

In sum, the primary schools, public or private, are: "to instruct the mass of our citizens in these, their rights, interests and duties, as men and citizens," and the proper subjects for this purpose are: "reading, writing and numerical arithmetic, the elements of mensuration (useful in so many callings) and the outlines of geography and history."

The objects of higher education, on the other hand, are, "for example":

> [1.] To form the statesmen, legislators and judges, on whom public prosperity and individual happiness are so much to depend;
>
> [5.] To expound the principles and structure of government, the laws which regulate the intercourse of nations, those formed municipally for our own government, and a sound spirit of legislation, which, banishing all arbitrary and unnecessary restraint on individual action, shall leave us free to do whatever does not violate the equal rights of another;

[4.] To harmonize and promote the interests of agriculture, manufactures and commerce, and by well informed views of political economy to give a free scope to the public industry;

[3.] To develop the reasoning faculties of our youth, enlarge their minds, cultivate their morals, and instill into them the precepts of virtue and order;

[2.] To enlighten them with mathematical and physical sciences, which advance the arts, and administer to the health, the subsistence, and comforts of human life;

[6.] And, generally, to form them to habits of reflection and correct action, rendering them examples of virtue to others, and of happiness within themselves.

These are the objects of that higher grade of education, the benefits and blessings of which the Legislature now propose to provide for the good and ornament of their country, the gratification and happiness of their fellow-citizens, of the parent especially, and his progeny, on which all his affections are concentrated.

I have numbered paragraphs so as to bring out the differences which Jefferson had evidently carefully considered. The objects are in each case:

CITIZENS	STATESMEN, LEGISLATORS, JUDGES
to conduct their own business,	to further public prosperity,
to learn to calculate,	to study science,
to improve in morality and ability,	to develop in reasoning and acquire virtue,
to function competently,	to form comprehensive opinions on the economy,
to know their rights and judge their officials,	to know the theory of governance,
to learn to live in society.	to reflect and act in an exemplary way.

The difference is clear: the citizen education is practical and turned toward private success, higher education theoretical and almost wholly directed to public service.

The first observation repeats what has already been pointed out: Jefferson thinks that citizens are "rendered by liberal education worthy to receive, and able to guard the sacred deposit of the rights and liberties of their fellow citizens.'' ("Bill of 1779.") Wide learning and theoretical studies are the prerequisite for officeholders. The opposition practical-liberal, which becomes so fluent in the nineteenth century, would have puzzled him, partly, of course, because he still adheres to some degree to the ancient distinction between *practical* and *productive*— between acting in the public realm and making things. What Jefferson thought this liberal education, capable of preparing republican rulers, ought to be, what elements of modernity, particularly of scientific and technical training he introduced, will be considered in the chapter on Tradition.

Now, was Jefferson's educational plan in fact aristocratic? It is a much-debated question because the answer to it seems to color the whole Founding.[37] Careful distinctions are therefore in order. With respect to the three-year primary schooling, the Jeffersonian proposal (never adopted) was in principle a modern tax-supported public-school system lacking only the feature of compulsory attendance. It is therefore, for example, quite understandable that in 1831 a sharply egalitarian call for public schooling could be dedicated to the shade of Jefferson.[38]

Higher education, on the other hand, was selective but by no means exclusive. The good and gifted students chosen would have come up through the selective middle schools; their whole course would have been publicly supported. However, those who had the financial means would be admitted merely by showing the prerequisites, a reading knowledge of Greek and Latin. Since the students at the university were destined for public affairs, this part of the plan might indeed be called aristocratic, in two senses: literally, as meaning *committed to the rule of the truly best*,—best, that is, by talent and character, and also, insofar as class and wealth did give easier access. On the other hand, the art of ruling that these students were to learn was, for Jefferson, the ability to represent the people and guard their rights and liberties. And so the education was also democratic, or at least for a democracy.

In truth, this political issue seems to me secondary to the educational question: Granting that learning is essential to republics, is an advanced formal education really the necessary condition for republican office? There have been rebellious populist denials of the Jeffersonian thesis: "Larning is of the gratest importance to the seport of a free government, and to prevent this the few are always crying up the advantages of costly collages, national acadimyes and grammer schooles." (William Manning, *The Key to Libberty*, 1798.)[39] There has been disproof in the person of Lincoln, whom I would call, not intending any hyperbole, the best-educated president to have sat in the White House (excluding neither Jefferson nor Wilson), or, at least, the best read, if by that may be meant one who reads well, not much. And this country has certainly not lately had conspicuous luck with "the best and the brightest" trained at the greatest universities. In sum, the dilemma of republican leadership is that learning is essential, but that a high-powered institutional education is not an absolutely trustworthy preparation for public office. What is wanted is a solid and deep liberal learning, which can be shared by citizens in and out of office.

Citizen-Philosopher. I shall be brief on this, the most interesting of all the oppositions respecting social utility, since my last chapter, on republican rationality, is largely devoted to it.

I want to note here only once more that Jefferson meant to institute at his university a philosophical doctrine called *Ideology*, a system derived from Bacon, Condillac, and Locke. Its attraction lay in part precisely in the fact that republican political principles seemed to be directly derivable from it.[40] The other early writers too were implicitly or explicitly concerned with the philosophical foundations of republican government, and they had just those articulate views on universal human concerns which are ordinarily called *philosophical*. The problems that their educational founding raises are: How can any determinate education, even if civil liberty is its object, admit perfect theoretical freedom? How can a designedly republican education leave scope for radical questions? And, more generally: How can any practical political education accommodate pure reflection?

ATTEMPTED RESOLUTION
OF THE PARADOX OF EDUCATIONAL UTILITY

Liberal Education

"All human beings by nature desire to know." More precisely: "All human beings hunger (*oregontai*) to know by their very nature." That is the first sentence of the founding work of first philosophy. (Aristotle *Metaphysics* 1.) The question of greatest consequence in an inquiry concerning educational utility is whether what Aristotle says is true.

Now, I think that it is both immediately and ultimately true. Aristotle adduces the pleasure everyone takes in sensing, particularly in seeing, the most synoptic of senses. And no pleasure is more perennial than that of the higher gossip, the activity of taking in and retailing human affairs. But human beings, and the young most readily, care as well and in a similar way for more arduous and more profound knowledge and for less accessible truth—it is not by accident that the words *theater* and *theory* are taken from the same verb, *to behold*. The blooms of this propensity are delicate, but the roots are hardy—in fact, indestructible. It may be tainted by the same conditions that expedite it: by the inward passion to shine before oneself, by the desire to be admired by those one admires, by sheer stubbornness, by the appetite for worldly recognition and reward. It may be obscured by *accidie*, that culpable ennui which is peculiarly a student's affliction, by the distraction of amusement, by indolence. And yet there will persist throughout a small, perhaps even vanishingly small, residue of the sheer desire to get to the truth of things. Teachers know and gamble on this underlying love of learning.

Now, if the desire for knowledge is really an aspect and even the essential aspect of human nature, then utilitarian education is a contradiction in terms, a perverse enterprise. Learning is naturally done for love, not for use; it is itself a mode of living, and not a mere means. On the other hand, a republic has a genuine public business, which is to provide for the possibility and protection of a good life in the worldly sense. Therefore, it has the responsibility of training its citizens for this purpose, and from this central fact all education will unavoidably derive a utilitarian cast, without needing to be the less an "enriching experience." From this point of view, it would indeed be "urgently important in American education today that the age-old distinction between education for living and education for making a living be discarded."[41]

Let me here formally introduce the traditional name for non-utilitarian education. It is called *liberal* education. The term has several significations. Literally it means simply "pertaining to freedom or to the free (*liberi*)." Since free children in particular are called *liberi* in Latin, it can be related to the upbringing of children who are to be free adults. It is often interpreted to mean "liberating,"—from the shackles of guardians or conventions.

But in its original use the term means, precisely, free from the bonds of utility:

> It is therefore not difficult to see that the young must be taught those useful arts that are indispensably necessary; but, those pursuits that are liberal (*eleutheron*) having been distinguished from those that are illiberal, it is clear that they should not be taught all the useful arts, and that they must participate in such among them as will not make the participant a philistine (*banauson*). [Aristotle, *Politics* VIII, 1337 b.]

Arts are *banausic*, or narrowly industrial, insofar as the worker does not realize his own ideas but by a mere routine produces a useful object in a mode that is the prototype of what Marx calls *alienation*. Even in antiquity the productive arts were not considered in themselves demeaning—Socrates called himself a stonemason and a descendant of the hero Daedalus the Craftsman. And in medieval and modern times the crafts and industrial trades have achieved every dignity, both as social goals and as forms of self-projection. (Jefferson, for example, thought the manual arts so worthy of encouragement that he wished to see the students at his university admitted to neighboring workshops.)[42] It is the glory of modernity to know that most kinds of productive work, including the service trades, can be carried on in a liberal spirit, intelligently and with relish. In fact, studies in job-satisfaction have shown what everyone in this country knows—that people invent ways to do freely and with gratification many jobs that would appear to have little scope or intrinsic interest.

Now, the point is this: All useful studies, like most useful work, can sometimes be pursued liberally. But the converse does not hold. All liberal learning is not useful, either not immediately or not at all, for there is a certain kind of learning that is not instrumental, except in a most oblique way. To do such learning or to leave it undone may, to be sure, have momentous worldly consequences. But we must bear in mind that "prior to its being a power, it is a good; that it is not only an instrument, but an end. I know well it may resolve itself into an art, and terminate in a mechanical process, and in tangible fruit; but it also may fall back upon that reason which informs it, and resolve itself into philosophy. In one case it is called useful knowledge, in the other liberal." (Newman, *The Idea of a University*, V, 6.) That is what the demand for the perfect conflation of liberal and vocational learning leaves out of consideration.

The Search for Ends

Discussion of what the learning might be that must be done for its own sake is left to the last chapter on Rationality; it will in any case have more intimacy and immediacy than instrumental learning. But there is one general aspect of it that belongs to the present argument.

We live in a Republic that does not attempt to provide happiness but to facilitate its pursuit; hence, all its ways are instrumental—our public realm is primarily one of means. Therefore, the inquiry into purposes, goods, ends, ought always to have been crucial; it will certainly be recognized to be so as our first long era of unreflectively exuberant production of means comes to its close.

Now, the study of ends, the question "What is good?" is the very culmination of all that learning which is "not only an instrument, but an end." The question will, to be sure, be asked out of the perplexities of living and with the hope of applying the answer—that is what gives it its driving impetus. Nonetheless, it often will and always should be done essentially for its own sake. For first, such a question is always asked from a sense of the insufficiency of the world of utility, some apprehension that the pursuit of the question itself is a surcease from instrumental activity. Second, the inquiry is not concerned with how to effect something but with what is good; it is not even concerned with that most elevated and peculiarly modern of utilitarianisms with which I began, the exercise and training of the mental tool. Now, errors in means can be relied on to become amply evident in the course of action, while mistakes about ends surface only in the long run, when it is too late. Therefore, such an inquiry had best be embarked on with the conviction that it is the truth and only the truth that is wanted, even at the risk of the search ending in a desperate conviction that there is for us no good end. Finally, the question conducts us into a realm of causal reasons, a realm of thought conceivably in itself worth dwelling on or in:

> For that knowledge is the most commanding and in command of those subservient to it, which understands for the sake of what each thing must be done, that is, the good in each case, and, in sum, what is best in the whole of nature.... It is through wondering that people both now and at first began to philosophize, wondering at the beginning about perplexities close at hand and then little by little advancing, and raising questions about greater matters.... Therefore if it was to escape ignorance that they philosophized, it is clear that they pursued knowledge for the sake of understanding and not for some utility. [*Metaphysics* I, 982b.]

In other words: As instrumental learning by its very intention neglects ends, so learning done for its own sake pursues them— the good is the implicit object of wonder.

Finally, the question will be asked: Can the Republic afford such an education, an education beyond utility? It is a brave part of the American understanding of the world to decree that where there is a natural right there the resources for its realization will be found. Is liberal education a natural right? By our founding charter we have three preeminent rights: "Life, Liberty, and the Pursuit of Happiness." Liberal education is not necessary to life. It is possible to live decently and comfortably without it, as the majority of citizens well know. It is, its name notwithstanding, not even necessary to liberty. That was evidently Jefferson's opinion: It is possible for a citizen "to know his rights; to exercise with order and justice those he retains; to choose with discretion the fiduciary of those he delegates" without a full course of liberal learning. It is, however, necessary (though not sufficient), or as nearly necessary as anything can be shown to be, for the pursuit of happiness. In brief, it is a near-essential preparation not for any life but for a good life. But a chance at a good life is not a mere desideratum in this Republic—it is indeed a right.

Tradition

2

THE DEVELOPMENT OF THE TRADITION

What Constitutes the Tradition

By *the tradition* I mean neither the old customs nor the recent routines, neither the sedimentary wisdom nor the petrified habits of communities. I mean, to begin with, *a collection of books.*

The possibility of a tradition is therefore dependent on the existence of an artificial memory, a way of storing the inventions of the imagination and the discoveries of the intellect externally: "So this excellent liquor of knowledge ... would soon perish and vanish to oblivion, if it were not preserved in books, traditions, conferences, and places appointed, as universities, colleges, and schools, for the receipt and comforting of the same." (Bacon, *Advancement of Learning*, II, Preface, 3.) Writing, that is, words of letters, are the principal such device, made possible by the tremendous fact that through words thought can appear as sound; there are also symbols of mathematics, notes of music, graphs, diagrams, models, images, each such notation being founded on some aspect of the world's intelligibility.[1] This external character of the tradition is crucially important, for it means not only that it can be materially annihilated, but—what is more problematical—that it can be physically extant and yet live a suspended life, lead an unappropriated existence. This great danger is set out in Plato's *Phaedrus*, in a fable that casts doubt on the blessings of the invention of writing, that "memory and wisdom drug." (274 e.) The Platonic dialogues are indeed attempts to forestall the philosophical "treatise," the authoritative treatment of a preset matter without any intrusive participants. Of course, they are nonetheless themselves writings. Indeed, even the perennial esoteric "unwritten doctrines" (*agrapha dogmata*) are defined against the written, esoteric tradition.

I use the word *tradition* for this bookish universe because at that time when people most ardently concerned themselves with its establishment and service, with the copying, collating, emending, editing, and interpreting of texts, the verb *tradere*, "to hand down," was literally and frequently used. For example, the humanist Vergerius writes:

> For literary monuments are in general good for much, and are especially necessary for the preserving of the memory of the ancients.... The memory of men, and what was transmitted from hand to hand, gradually slips away, and scarcely survives the span of one man. Only what is consigned to books remains perpetually, unless perhaps pictures, or marble sculptures or poured metal are able to accomplish some such thing.... But what is handed down [*traditur*] in letters not only expresses what was done but also records the conversations and expresses the reflections of men. And if it is circulated in many copies, it cannot easily perish, if only worth attach to the speech. [*On the Good Morals and Studies of Youth*, ca. 1400.][2]

By the tradition I mean, further, the books of the West, ancient, medieval, and modern, omitting, however, the post-biblical Jewish and the Arabic writings—a major lacuna—because of my ignorance and their present inaccessibility. By the same token, I omit all reference to Eastern learning; I do not even know whether it forms a tradition in the sense I am trying to formulate. For what sharply defines the bookish Western tradition as a handing down is that it is acquired by study. That is to say, it is appropriated by a set, episodic application of the intellect and the sensibility, which is carried on in distinction from the world's business. It can therefore be both institutionalized in "places of leisure," that is, in schools (from *scholē*, Greek for *leisure*) or done at private leisure, in isolation. Furthermore, books of papyrus, parchment, or paper can be taken more lightly and carried about more nonchalantly than learning had "by heart," through a "way." Western published learning is thus eminently portable: A copy of Locke may be carried by an anthropologist into an African jungle village and consulted on a day in need of edification.[3] I have a half-informed suspicion that the Eastern learning is not approachable through a program of study *ad libitum*, but by a living discipline—that it is not a matter of informing the intellect but of training the soul, not *mathēsis* but *askēsis*, as the Greeks would say. And, conversely, it is precisely because the Western learning is essentially not a training for the soul or a way of life but theory, that it is continually and problematically ambitious to become practical.

In the same vein, the Western tradition is eminently and deliberately accessible. The books are meant to explain themselves, even (or particularly) the most abstruse of them. For example, Kant prefaces the *Critique of Pure Reason* with a comment on its intelligibility, in which he contends that his text is just what it must be to be understood. (A xvii.) In fact, besides a certain inexhaustibility of meaning and elegance of formulation, self-sufficiency of presentation has always been a criterion for the assumption of a book into the traditional canon.

The tradition is not, it follows, an influence to be atmospherically absorbed, but a group of works to be immediately and crisply confronted, without interpretative intervention or predigestion.

A very tentative word should here be said about the effect of the republic of letters on other communities, though naturally this whole inquiry is concerned with that embarrassing matter. It used to be more easily conceded than it is now that the saying Bacon cites in *Of Studies* holds: *Abeunt studia in mores*, "Studies go to conduct." But even if it were agreed that books shape men intermediately, it would still be a question whether they do so ultimately—whether they form affairs or follow them. The power of learning to impinge on the world of action for the better, a power it sometimes disdains but usually seeks, is yet a further problem, most acutely raised by Plato's brazen claim that there will be "no surcease from evils" until "the political power and philosophy coincide." (*Republic* 473 d.) This latter aspect, which is, more immediately, the question of reforming the world through education, has been touched on and will again be considered. But as far as the mere power of such learning is concerned, aside from the desirability of the results, let me mention only two overwhelmingly important cases. The most sagacious observer of the most exemplary modern upheaval attributed it peculiarly to the activity of the "men of letters." (Tocqueville, *The Old Regime and the French Revolution*, III, 1.) The second case is that marriage of the liberal and mechanical arts which governs modern life under the name of technology. These cases put the power of Western *theorizing* to affect and alter the world beyond question—the problem is the efficacy of *education* in reaching and improving human beings.

Now, this tradition, precisely because when it is truest to itself it aims at truth-telling rather than at a training of the soul, is quarrelsome. It is by no means merely a happily heritable treasure trove: *traditio* literally means both transmission and betrayal. Nor is this quarrel simply a matter of *Sic et Non*,[4] the level back-and-forth of a "Yes and No" concerning set theses. The tradition has, to catch a mystery in a term, a *development*. Therefore it has beginnings—or perhaps, rather conversely, it has a development because it once was not. I think that everyone who has occupied himself with these first appearances has a sense that they are inexplicable—miraculous, one might say—as indeed the existence of the whole has in it something of an unaccountable dispensation.

There is, then, a first and earliest Western poet—possibly he was the first to have the benefit of alphabetical writing—who assumed into his epics all the earlier rhapsodies.[5] There is a progenitor of philosophy, "Father" Parmenides (Plato *Sophist* 241 d), who made *being* the determining theme of what was later called metaphysics. But Homer's tales and their sequels are perennially and competitively retold, by Aeschylus or Virgil or Racine or Joyce. And Parmenides already had an elder antagonist, Heraclitus, whom he chastised for asserting that "to be and not to be are the same" (Fragment 6), thus joining issue on the first and perpetual metaphysical question.

So also the Book par excellence, the Bible, which is a beginning and begins with a beginning, becomes the Old Covenant through the advent of another, a New Testament (Paul, *Hebrews* 8:13), which, however, derives its legitimacy from its forerunner. Hence, the whole subsequent Christian tradition is intensely preoccupied with the irruption into time of the utterly new that is yet also a fulfillment of the old.

So, once begun, the tradition, viewed for just a moment in a thoroughly pernicious way, as a piece of continuous conceptual protoplasm, has in it a principle of motion that is equally a principle of continuity and of selection. Once a beginning is made, every contributor grows on the ground of the tradition. The founder of Christianity at the age of twelve sat among the rabbis; the founder of Protestantism was a monk; the founder of modern physics, a student of Aristotle. But in wishing articulately to supersede his antecedent antagonist, each new member memorializes him and thus bestows a more potent confirmation of importance than any critical labor could confer.

Within the tradition there are certain perennial issues that are peculiarly connected to transmission itself, to the question: Which constituents are worthy of being preserved and taught, and which ought to be suppressed or superseded? One such issue is "a certain ancient quarrel" between philosophy and poetry (in which philosophy is usually the vociferous aggressor: Plato, *Republic* X 607 b; Plutarch *How to Study Poetry*), a distinction that later hardens into that of fact and fiction. Another is that opposition of philosophy and faith, in which faith attacks. ("Beware lest any man spoil you through philosophy"; Paul, *Colossians* 2:8.) Again there is the antagonism of reason and revelation (most subtly waged for reason by Spinoza, *Theologicopolitical Treatise*); of reason and authority; of the old and the new science (as conveyed in the titles of Galileo's and Vico's *"New" Sciences* and Bacon's *"Novum" Organum*). And above all, there is the great Battle Between the Ancients and Moderns (a comically literal version of which is depicted by

Swift in his "Battle of the Books Held One Friday"; the outcome remains in doubt due to a lacuna in the manuscript). For my part, I think that were this contest ever finally abandoned the Western tradition would have ended. These then are some of the peculiar quarrels that both move the tradition and perennially recollect it.

The Positions Respecting the Tradition

The positions people have taken toward this inheritance have varied between the poles of *tabula rasa* and perfect piety.[6] There are those who want to make or who admire a clean slate, an absolutely fresh, even savage, beginning, and others who preach and practice adherence to texts without an iota's alteration. Both positions are feasible, and people have lived by them. The vigorous and virtuous barbarians of many episodes have been admired and imitated by the respective Romans whose city they have sacked, though these barbarians have usually found it an unsettling elevation to sit on so precious a midden heap. We ourselves rightly admire the crisp intelligence of the scientific neobarbarians among us. (Real primitives are, of course, a much more delicate article that we need only to study to ravage.)[7] Perfect piety, on the other hand, need not be desiccated. It does service as civilization's holding pattern, and it can also produce a certain quiescent, self-enfolded distillation of learning that is graced by a deep simplicity. I am thinking of some of the modest and self-assured medieval writings on teaching and learning; for example, a teacher says to his pupil:

> Now, then, these are the steps which you are seeking. May you always be as ardent to ascend them as you are just now curious to be shown them: grammar, rhetoric, dialectic, arithmetic, geometry, music, and astronomy. With those the philosophers occupy themselves in leisure and at business. Through them they become more illustrious than consuls, more famous than kings; through them they are praised in everlasting remembrance. [Alcuin, *Grammar*, ca. 800.][8]

In between these problematic extremes lie the other positions. To make a beginning in placing them, I shall employ five terms that have, I confess, all the operational repulsiveness of any constructed concept: *Origination*, *Canonization*, *Renovation*, *Repudiation*, and *Inundation*.

These terms correspond crudely to the usual designations for epochs of world or intellectual history, some of which are, to be sure, actually named after a prevailing position with respect to the tradition: Antiquity; Late Antiquity and the Middle Ages; the Renaissance; the Age of Reason and the Enlightenment; and contemporary Modernity.

As an exact description of any time such categories are, as a matter of course, worthless, and not merely because it is in principle perverse to wish to articulate "the thought of a time," for what is caught in such a hyperindividual characterization is precisely *thoughtless* thought, that is, prevailing opinion. Rather, the fit is not precise enough: already in Greek antiquity, while the tradition was originating, venerable ancients were distinguished from voluble moderns (in Aristophanes' *Frogs*, Aeschylus and Euripides); in the Middle Ages, the time of canonization, there occurred both so many distinguishable renaissances as to prove an embarrassment to the historian,[9] as well as outright rebellion: "What does the old donkey want? Why does he feed us the sayings and doings of the ancients? We have our knowledge out of ourselves. We, the young do not recognize the ancients!" (Sorrowfully cited by John of Salisbury, 11th century.)[10] During the Renaissance there was much exuberant canonmaking and revising as new texts were recovered and old ones discredited; it was a time preoccupied with "great books" lists (Vives, *On the Transmission of the Disciplines*, I, vi.).[11] And during the great repudiation, powerful defenders of classical learning were found even among the leaders of the Enlightenment (Diderot, in his *Plan of a University*.)[12] And, finally, it is precisely in our time, when the tradition is all but swamped, that the most deadly serious attempts to recover both the poetic and the philosophical tradition are made—if only to exploit the former for *parody*, "the illusionistic play with dead forms" (Thomas Mann, *Doktor Faustus*, ch. XXV), and to reappropriate the latter toward its ultimate *demolition* (Heidegger, *Being and Time*, ch. II, 6: "'The Project of a Destruction of Ontology'").

Clearly, then, my terms do no more than catch the historical drift rather crudely, though they name a possible position precisely enough. Let me sketch in some detail.

Origination. What is, from the present point of view, characteristic of this situation is that the Greeks themselves, who were in it, needed no languages or translations to read their own classics, and that therefore the education of their young included no language study; in fact, I know of no classical Greek author who admits to speaking any barbaric babble. This fact about the Greeks is triumphantly pointed out by the American educational reformers like Franklin, for whom language learning was a major concern. To a Roman student, Greek was recommended by Quintilian (I, i, 12) for study as a first language, both because Latin learning was regarded as derivative from Greek and because Latin could be expected to be learned naturally. The humanist educators found this order impractical because, as the vernacular became legitimate, Latin was itself a learned language. In modern times, at last, the mother tongue was, thanks in part to Locke, taught in the schools. Consequently, Greek became the third language, if taught at all (though the earlier order survived as a special pedagogical device—J. S. Mill's father put him to Greek five years before Latin, when he was three).[13]

But it is not only in the obvious respect of language that the ancients had a more immediate relation to their classics than do the readers of later times. There evidently never developed that sense of remoteness from their own authors which prevails among us. *Time was never of the essence*: The age of which Homer tells came seven hundred years before the Athens of Pericles, and Homer himself two hundred and fifty years. Yet Homer was, then and after, the undisputed school author, with no sense of anything antiquated or even antique about him. Quarrels there were—between poets and poets, and poets and philosophers, and philosophers and sophists. The cycle of liberal studies was deprecated as unsuitable to men of affairs (Isocrates, *Antidosis* 262). But never, as far as I know, was a major author set aside as being *no longer* worth while. This first position, then, is one of immediacy. (I do not even reckon in, because it requires too great an imaginative labor, what it might have meant to be a contemporary assisting at the birth of some of the founding works of the tradition, how it must have felt to hear them and to take them in without a written text, as Attic audiences seem to have been capable of doing.)

Canonization. In late antiquity, in the fifth, sixth, and seventh centuries, compendia of the classical encyclopedic education were produced, settling not only the names, number, and connection of the liberal arts (namely, the ones cited by Alcuin as quoted above), but intending to convey all their matter as well. This matter thus became a fixed, finite, attainable learning with which philosophy in the broad sense was understood to be coextensive. The chief such works, whose main sources were Quintilian and the lost books of Varro, are Martianus Capella's *Marriage of Philology and Mercury* (ca. 425), a perfectly baroque allegory that became the chief schoolbook of the Middle Ages; Boethius' treatises on the *quadrivium*, a term he introduced (early sixth century; the term *trivium* does not occur until the ninth century); and Cassiodorus, *System of the Sacred and Worldly Arts* (sixth century).[14]

A fateful division was now reinforced between the "three-way" of rational arts (*trivium*) and the "four-way" of mathematical arts (*quadrivium*), the arts of speech and the arts of things. The humanists of the Renaissance were to project the trivium into modernity by opposing it to divine learning in the form of the literary *studia humanitatis*. When, next, the study of nature came to the fore, the medieval division assumed its modern form, our *humanities* and *natural sciences*. Their antagonistic confrontation was first given its standard modern exposition by Vico in his essay "On the Rationale of Study in Our Time," which is a defense of the humanities against the encroachments of the Cartesian method, that is, the application of algebra to nature. During medieval times, however, when the arts most flourished, it was not against the *quadrivium* that the arts of human expression wanted defending—an unthinkable proposition—but against the notion that one might attain them as a gift rather than by a studious pursuit; this was John of Salisbury's project in the *Metalogicon*, the greatest of all defenses of the *trivium*. Until quite modern times, one or the other of the trivial arts was the secular object of the mainstream of all study: rhetoric—that is, eloquence—for men of affairs; logic for schoolmen; grammar (literally, *literature*) for humanists.

Eventually, the identification of the encyclopedic arts with philosophy was retracted; the arts were found "not adequately to divide theoretical philosophy." Thomas Aquinas pronounced them, as they were for Plato and Aristotle, ancillary, merely roads to the higher sciences such as physics, that is, natural philosophy, and theology.[15] Similarly, in the universities the professional faculties of law, medicine, and theology came to stand beside the arts faculty.

Aslant of the arts, as it were, there were the canonized authors (*auctores*), writers who possessed authority (*auctoritas*). An author could in earlier times be regarded as a mere name "which tells nothing about the art." (Conrad of Hirsau, ca. 1100.)[16] That is to say, the world of learning was fully fixed with respect to matter and the authors merely contributed a convenient text. The eventual recovery of the authors' originating authority marked a great ferment in this world of fixed matter.

Renovation. *Renovatio*, "renewal," is the term given to this position in its most exemplary period, the Renaissance. During this "resurrection of letters" the tradition was refurbished through an enormous scholarly servicing of texts. The universities began to teach Greek; for example, Thomas More wrote a long letter to the faculty of Oxford University, defending and encouraging Greek studies (29 March 1518). What is more, all manner of people learned Greek on their own, even in old age: Gargantua writes a long and loving letter in praise of the new learning to his boy Pantagruel, in which he confesses to the Greek studies of his old age (II, 8). But the productive spirit of this or any renewal is best given by an early proponent, Petrarch, because he conveys the resonances of this recovery. The ancients and moderns, he says, are like fathers and sons, different in every detail; and yet "a shadow, as it were, and a something our painters call an air" is common to them. Then he puts briefly and perfectly the principle of Renaissance production: "per litteras provocati, pariunt in seipsis" ["incited by texts, they gave birth for themselves"] (*Epistolares Familiares*). The downfall of each such exhilarating episode, always feared even at its greatest moments, is imitation, pedantry, formalism—in short, yet another scholasticism. I think that renovation is the mode most essential to the life of the tradition, and I think, too, that we are so situated as to be capable of no other novelty.

Repudiation. The proper modern beginning of this position is to be found in Bacon's *Advancement of Learning*, whose deep-laid schemes, future-fraught cleverness, and coolly balanced rationality overshadow everything that comes after. Its full ascendancy belongs to the period called by its own participants "The Age of Reason" and "The Enlightenment," whose American aspects I intend to treat in the next section.[17] But now the tradition came under decided and competent attack. The transmission or *tradition* of knowledge was discredited in favor of the *advancement* and *diffusion* of knowledge—these were the new key terms. Communities of learning yielded to agencies of research, whose exemplar was depicted in Bacon's *New Atlantis*.

Let me outline those features of this mode which seem to me distinctive.

First, a final decision was felt to have been reached in the quarrel, now apprehended as very weary, between the ancients and the moderns. Modernity was to prevail. *Modern* is a term going back to the sixth century,[18] coined from *modo*, "just now." Just-nowness, contemporaneity, that is, a productive complex of secularism and science, of care for and competence in the *present* world—"present" in every sense—won the day. The moderns felt themselves to be wiser in the ways of the world than the ancients: "*Antiquitas saeculi juventus mundi* [Temporal antiquity is worldly immaturity]—These times are the ancient times, when the world is ancient, and not those which we account ancient *ordine retrogrado*, by a computation backward from ourselves." (Bacon, *Advancement*, I, v, 1.) In time there naturally surfaced a strain of breezy vandalism. Malebranche announced: "It is useless enough to those who live at present to know whether a man called Aristotle ever lived." (*The Search After Truth*.) But by and large it was a grave and responsible superiority that characterized the bearing of modern authors toward the ancients.

A second feature was the pervasive triumph of the old cry: *res non verba*, "things, not words."[19] This was a revulsion against book learning, against words both as notions and as utterances, in favor of real, literally "thingish," preoccupations. From the point of view of study, this meant that the young "be instructed in several Sciences . . . and all other Parts of Knowledge of Things that fall under the Senses. . . . For there, if we would take the true way, our Knowledge should begin . . . and not in the abstract Nations of *Logick* and *Metaphysicks*." (Locke, *Thoughts*, 166.) Hence, texts were to be complemented, or even supplanted by instruments: "But certain it is, that unto deep, fruitful, and operative study of many sciences, especially Natural Philosophy and Physic, books be not the only instrumentals . . . for we see spheres, globes, astrolabes, maps, and the like." (Bacon, *Advancement*, II, Preface, 10.) At the same time, early and long learning of Latin and Greek came under attack, and first by no scorner of ancient learning, for Milton considered that language, too, is in the service of the real: "Language is but the instrument conveying things useful to be known." (*Of Education*.) Indeed, there were attacks on all the "Knowledge of Tongues" which "beareth a great noise in the world" but steals time from the learning of *things*.[20] The change in the use of the word *encyclopedia* is revealing here; it no longer meant, as it did from antiquity, the current cycle of philosophically determined liberal arts, but a comprehensive introduction to worldly learning (for example, for Comenius, a great pedagogical proponent of "things, not words"), which was, finally, by Diderot's enterprise, reduced to a "Reasoned

Dictionary of the Sciences, Arts and Trades." (d'Alembert, *Preliminary Discourse to the Encyclopedia of Diderot.*)

As always, there was a kind of reactionary pendant to this feature, which issued in something really shocking, a mischievous attack on learning by the learned themselves. It is to be seen in the disingenuous destructiveness of Rousseau's *Discourse on the Question Proposed by the Academy of Dijon: Has the Restoration of the Sciences and the Arts Tended to Purify Morals?* and its artfully negative answer. And it is seen again in the Satan-seeking frivolity of the German national poem, whose body begins with these scandalous lines:

> So now I have, in the sweat of my brow
> Completed philosophy, physic and law,
> And to my regret, theology too.
> Well, here I stand, poor fool that I am,
> And am as wise as when I began.
> [Goethe, *Faust*, II. 354-59.]

These works condemn the tradition of learning, one for corrupting virtue and the other for dessicating the passions.[21] They were written with artful wit, but too often read with artless abandon. The European rebellion against learning was, however, I think, significantly distinct from the aboriginal American variety. That latter attack, at least until the temporary Europeanization of the sixties, came from the faithful, the philistines, and the bumptious egalitarians of the perennial "Davy Crockett line."[22] I mention it because it played an important and not always unhealthy extratraditional role in American education.

The third ingredient of the mode of repudiation was that final yielding of authority to evidence with which I mean to deal more directly in my last chapter. The characteristic view was, "so let great authors have their due, as time, which is the author of authors, be not deprived of his due, which is, further and further to discover the truth." (Bacon, *Advancement*, I, iv, 12.) By authority I do not in the least mean the trusting *ipse dixit* of the canonizing phase (which was, moreover, never so fatuous as later windmill fighters pretend). I mean, rather, a habit of respect for tried texts, partly out of a regard for the consensus that has preserved them, partly from an ingenuous expectation that some words may convey wisdom. In the mode of evidence, on the other hand, the expectation is that things may prove words wrong and that everyone must be ever ready to exercise immediate and decided judgment, even if it takes the form of judiciously withholding the same.

Again, there was an evidently inevitable aberration in the form of the violent litany of anticlericalism. For example, the usually pacific Jefferson's last public communication, regretting his inability to assist at the celebration in Washington of the Declaration's fiftieth anniversary, managed to present the revolutionaries as bursting "the chains under which monkish ignorance and superstitution had persuaded them to bind themselves." The consequences of this strain, too, are to be reckoned with in American education.

All three features together are found in Bacon, Locke, and Newton (Jefferson's "trinity of the three greatest men the world had ever produced, . . . without any exception") and in their French expositors (whom he studied, if anything, more closely, at least in later life). These then "laid the foundation of those superstructures which have been raised in the physical and moral sciences."[23] If Descartes had been included they would indeed have comprised the founders of modernity in general; as it is, they are the specific sources of the repudiation of the tradition in America.

Inundation. Concerning our own condition with respect to the tradition, I only outline what everyone knows. First, there has occurred a simple swamping of the tradition by rival productions disproportionate in volume and propagation, and deliberately or unconsciously intended to displace it. Or perhaps it is more accurate to say that the tradition itself is running riot with success. In any case, under these circumstances the time-honored principles of election and confirmation cease to work, until it is next to impossible, even in the privacy of one's own judgment, to determine whether the formation is in fact continuing. To compound the confusion, in the last century and a half the books of canonical stature have nearly all proclaimed the ending—in consummation or catastrophe—of the Western tradition. Hence, the "classics" become, so to speak, carefully listed specimen survivals, stowed away in an ark floating upon the face of the waters where they are "worked on," rather than read, by a skeleton crew. For the public, they acquire at best the unregarded expensive charm of those colonial relics at the bottom of canyons of business buildings that can sometimes be seen in eastern cities. At the same time, although contemporary production is massive, the proportion of excellence to quantity probably decreases; the items neutralize rather than address each other; the most remarkable works are often too technical to speak to the lay world and are endlessly bowdlerized. Mere massiveness, muchness, manyness, becomes a determinant of learning; yet it appears to be easier for a camel to pass through the eye of a needle than that all that "information" should go over into the realm of wisdom.

Second, there is the almost universal view we have of ourselves as living not merely in a time of unusual change—that view is by now a good half-millennium old—but of changing change, of exponential change, that is, technically, change such that the rate of change changes in proportion to the accumulated consequences of previous change. "Life and education become dynamic" and "show an accelerating pace of change"—these Toynbee phrases are the stock-in-trade of our reflections on ourselves. It is a view largely inspired by the first factor, the enormity of our accumulations. For not only is mere quantitative increase understood as qualitative change, but the illusion of newness is reinforced by the eclipse of the old—for those who have not heard of what was, what is is always the unheard-of: what is an innovation to a sociologist is apt to be to a historian a revival. Hence, the mere formal fact of change begins to appear as part of the essence of things. Under these circumstances much writing is done in the spirit of those repair manuals for complex aircraft with continually obsolescent circuitry, which erase themselves after a certain time; it is intentionally ephemeral. And with respect to the already established tradition, the problem of "relevance" becomes acute—significantly, the terminus of the relation is rarely given, presumably because it is indeterminable in so fast a flux. I have already argued to the contrary of this notion of ourselves as living in a time of change, claiming that our situation is almost too compacted for true motion. What is more, I believe this truth to be an open secret.

Third, there is prevalent in the academy an understanding of history such that it absorbs the tradition, that is to say, it is conceived that history is a complex of "periods" that have an all-determining, suprapersonal character, expressing itself in Society or as Spirit. Hence, texts cease to be original human utterances and instead become historical evidence for "the intellectual outlook of human society" or "the current thought of the epoch."[24] Nietzsche is eloquent about the anesthetizing pedagogical effect of this "malady of history" on young students, who are made to live in a "culture which is not a real culture but a knowledge about culture." (*The Uses and Abuses of History*, sec. VI.) The academy tends to treat the tradition taxidermically.

Now, although Inundation is our own condition and plays an overwhelming role in our education, I shall address myself in the next section to Repudiation. The reason is the very circumstance that our situation has so much of brute fact in it, is so much the foretellable, indeed foretold, consequence of deliberate choices, particularly rejections, made in the early times of the Republic, which coincide with the beginning of proximate modernity. In other words, the root issues were more accessible then; they sowed the wind, we reap the whirlwind.

TRADITION AND EDUCATION IN THE EARLY REPUBLIC

Classical and Modern Learning

A review of Jefferson's own classical learning seems the best beginning,[25] for it naturally affected his educational plans, and it is, though not standard, revealing. It is the exemplary case of the American sequel to the battle between the ancients and the moderns, whose educational aspects had been the subject of an extensive controversy, begun in earnest by Locke and carried on with spirit and elegance—all the protagonists being classically educated—through the eighteenth century. (What comes after is increasingly a rear-guard action; Thoreau's chapter "Reading" in *Walden* is a brave example.) The typical questions are whether and for what and by whom classical languages and authors are to be read: whether they produce public-spirited men of affairs or "musty mortals" in libraries; whether they are to be looked to as sources of refined taste and elegant language or of practical wisdom and experienced judgment; whether they are appropriate only to gentlemen destined for public and private action or for the sons of rising tradesmen. A spirited compendium of all these topics is to be found in a work "much esteem'd" in America, particularly by Franklin, Fordyce's *Dialogues Concerning Education*.[26]

The most practical part of this issue concerns the study of ancient languages in the schools. It was a matter of much interest to Jefferson, who was an avid amateur classicist of a breadth to eclipse the crimped professionalism of most modern classicists. In a passage containing one of the rare references to his father he wrote, "I enjoy Homer in his own language infinitely beyond Pope's translation of him, and both beyond the dull narrative of the same event by Dares Phrygius; and it is an innocent enjoyment. I thank on my knees Him who directed my early education, for having put into my possession this rich source of delight: and I would not exchange it for anything I could then have acquired, and have not since acquired." (To Priestley, 27 January 1800.) And over and over, he expresses his love for Homer beyond all other poets: "I suspect we are left at last with Homer and Virgil, perhaps with Homer alone." (*Thoughts on English Prosody*.) Now, to read Homer is mandatory for classicists, to love him not unheard of, but wade through imitators like Dares Phyrgius and Quintus Smyrnaeus—!

Naturally and justly, Jefferson comported himself as a judge of style, of translations, of pronunciation, as a textual critic, and as an explicator of texts and terms; for example, like Goethe, he tried his hand at rendering the term *logos* of the Gospel of John.[27]

His advice, whether to his nephew Peter Carr (10 August

1785), or to history professors at the University of Virginia (25 October 1825), was always to read texts, even historical works, in the original "and not in translations." What is more, he regarded such accomplishments as peculiarly appropriate to Americans. He made the eyebrow-raising claim that "ours are the only farmers who can read Homer" (To Crèvecoeur, 15 January 1787), and he certainly thought the educated ought to do so. "The learning of Greek and Latin, I am told, is going into disuse in Europe. I know not what their manners and occupations may call for: but it would be very ill-judged in us to follow their example in this instance." (*Notes on Virginia*, Qu. XIV.) The pedagogical reason, partly a pretext, I think, is that children should not be forced to be men too soon, that there is a time in childhood when the memory and not the judgment should be exercised, and that this is the very time for studying Greek and Latin. Language, he observed, echoing Milton, is not science, though it is the "instrument for the attainment of science." Primary education was to be devoted largely to a first (and for some, final) study of history—Greek, Roman, English, and American. ("Bill of 1779.") History, too, "exercises principally the memory. Reflection also indeed enters, but not in a laborious degree." (To Thomas Mann Randolph, 27 August 1786; compare Locke, *Thoughts Concerning Education*, 166.) At about fifteen, a second, more serious, original course of reading, including Herodotus, Thucydides, and Justin, was to be undertaken. (To Carr, 19 August 1785.) The university course, where Greek and Latin is assumed, was to include the more obviously sophisticated authors like Suetonius and Tacitus as well as monographs and moderns. (25 October 1825.)

Now, the true object of the concentration on antique history was to prevent early Bible study. (*Notes*, Qu. XIV.) At the age when what is learned is learned "by heart," the political lessons of history are to displace for pupils the religious dogmas of the Bible: "History by apprising them of the past will enable them to judge of the Future." (*Notes*, Qu. XIV.) History will effect this development by teaching pupils to recognize the "germ of corruption and degeneracy." It is selective, vicarious political experience, an "essentially necessary" improvement of the mind, if the ambitions of rulers are to be defeated. History, in a rather dubious sense, is *the* republican study. (Some of the early republican writers are quite forthright about selecting the readings to strengthen republican sensitivity.) The point here, however, is that access to history's higher reaches is thought to be through the ancient languages, which are consequently tools of republican learning.[28]

Accordingly, no educational scheme ever devised by Jefferson omitted this study. The "Bill for the More General Diffusion of Knowledge" of 1779 and the plan of schooling communicated to Peter Carr (7 September 1814) both provided for Greek and Latin at the grammar and general schools (that is, roughly, secondary school and college). In the "Rockfish Gap Report," they were termed the "passage of entrance" into the University of Virginia; in the same document a chair of advanced Greek, Latin, and Hebrew was proposed.

Now what, in sum, besides the ability to read ancient historians, is the use of these studies?[29] The answer is explicitly given in a reply to an inquiry from a Harvard latinist, John Brazer (24 August 1819): "The utilities we derive from the remains of the Greek and Latin languages are, first, as models of pure taste in writing. To these we are certainly indebted for the rational and chaste style of modern composition"; second, "the luxury of reading the Greek and Roman authors in all the beauties of their originals"—here Jefferson again thanks his father for this "innocent and elegant luxury," which comforts the ennui of old age; third, the "stores of real science deposited and transmitted us" in those languages: again history, then ethics, but also the "real" subjects of mathematics and natural history.

But even while he expatiates on the subject he makes its matter evaporate: First, Greek and Latin are said to shape style. Now, it is probably true that rational writing and classical learning often go in tandem, but my guess is that it is because those who cherish language learn Greek and Latin. Be that as it may, classical learning is demonstrably neither sufficient nor necessary to good English.[30] Good philologists have written bad vernacular, and men of little Latin and less Greek have written the greatest English, even consciously contrasting Latinate and Anglo-Saxon diction. I cite a famous example:

> No, this my hand will rather
> The multitudinous seas incarnadine,
> Making the green one red.
>
> [*Macbeth*, II, ii.]

And Lincoln, without Latin, had a similar ability, as a comparison of the Anglo-Saxon Gettysburg Address with the Latinate First Inaugural shows.

Jefferson's argument belongs to that old humanist strain which claims, rather obscurely, that language studies are good for the soul. Locke is responsible for spreading its counterpart for the study of mathematics with the claim that it can be used to "settle in the mind a habit of reasoning closely and in train." (*Conduct of the Understanding*, 7.) These unfounded assertions, that a certain training is improving to the mind, always finally discredit such studies, since everyone knows that, as classicists are not always stylists, so mathematicians are not otherwise particularly rational people (though the converse often holds). To be sure, the study of Latin and Greek prevents certain barbarisms, but if that prissy good is all that can be gained, we may confidently expect a hard-working people to do without the "dead" languages.

There is, I think, a more compelling argument for these studies, at least for preserving some knowledge of classical languages in the community. It is that however oblivious of these tongues *we* may be, our *language* continues to speak Greek and Latin. But as access to them decays, our speech begins to bear a dead weight of unmeant meanings. It is no cure simply to look up words in a dictionary, since the mere etymology is quite lifeless without some context. Now these vestigal meanings debilitatingly fetter our thinking with hidden determinations. That is, at least in part, why Tocqueville entitles a chapter "The Study of Greek and Latin Literature is Peculiarly Useful in Democratic Communities." (*Democracy in America*, II, bk. 1, xv.) As he says, "There is no more wholesome medicine for the mind."

Jefferson's second utility—note the obligatory utilitarianism—is the delight the classics give. They are both innocent and
a luxury—devastating praise to present to the adventurous and
enterprising young, for whom an innocent enjoyment merely
denotes an impotent pleasure. Also, this view must have been a
source of the recurrent feeling in earlier America that a classical
education is the invidiously distinctive "accomplishment" of
the idle overprivileged, a gentlemen's amusement.

Besides, the reduction of any learning to a matter of taste
puts it in a very delicate position. To be sure, the classicizing
taste seemed solidly entrenched during the early Republic. One
proof is the fact that Jefferson, who despised local colonial
building but gazed at the Maison Carrée "like a lover at his
mistress," succeeded in having it adapted, in a modified version, as the model for the state capitol at Richmond. And as
assembly houses were "capitols," so schoolyards were "cam-
puses." It was even suggested that the Olympic Games be
reinstituted: "Having acted upon Greek principles you should
have Greek exercises."[31] But the classics are never more triflingly
read than in classicizing settings, a popular taste passes away,
and even a great man's private relish cannot long maintain its
influence. In short, Jefferson's second utility has very precarious
persuasiveness.

The final use of the classics to Americans is to come from the
matter they convey: "The classical languages are a solid basis for
most, and an ornament to all sciences." I have commented in
the first chapter on the significance of this opposition of *useful*
and *ornamental*—the distinction between substance and adjunct. Here the important claim is that the classics do convey
some substance, are *real*. What matter do they convey? Here are
Jefferson's headings and their limitations.

There is, as observed above, history. But whether history, and
particularly ancient history, can really serve the didactic purpose
Jefferson assigns it was even then the matter of a deep debate.
There was another American Founder, that preeminent anti-
Jeffersonian Hamilton, who considered the ancient case precisely
incommensurable with the American—the ancients were fero-
cious and honorable; we are pacific and reasonable. Tocqueville,

too, finds that the ancient republics cannot be compared to the American; he is tempted to burn his books so as to come to a novel case with novel ideas only.[32]

Next comes ethics. Jefferson's observations on ancient ethics occur in the context of a definition of the difference between the pagan philosophers on the one hand and the Jews and Jesus on the other. The philosophers' "precepts are related chiefly to ourselves.... In this branch of philosophy they were really great," but "in developing our duty to others, they were short and defective," for they taught justice and friendship, but not, as did Jesus, benevolence and charity. Now this observation is very perceptive. Virtue, justice, and friendship toward fellow citizens are *the* classical terms, which, under the influence of enlightened Christianity, are transformed into "duty, charity and benevolence to the whole circle of mankind" (to Rush, 21 April 1803)—substitutions ultimately world-shaking in their consequences. But if the latter are the nondefective terms of morality, then morality is not primarily a philosophical matter: "The precepts of philosophy . . . laid hold of actions only. He pushed his scrutinies into the heart of man." In contradiction to the Socratic dictum, Jefferson's modern virtue is not knowledge; it is feeling, and lectures in moral philosophy are "lost time." "He who made us would have been a pitiful bungler, if he had made the rule of our moral conduct a matter of science." A ploughman will do better than a professor in a moral case. And so will a novelist—the writings of Sterne offer the best course in morality (to Carr, 10 August 1787)—indeed, the libertarian pathos and the tolerant benevolence of the *Sentimental Journey* strike a recognizably Jeffersonian note. Therefore, in brief, the pagan classics have nothing truly valuable to offer in ethics.

Next comes mathematics. A powerful argument can (and will) indeed be made for reading ancient mathematical texts, on the grounds that ancient synthetic mathematics is qualitatively different from modern Cartesian analysis, and that a comparative study makes it possible to raise radical questions concerning the nature of mathematical objects. That, of course, is not Jefferson's purpose. In fact, Jefferson had too high an opinion of modern mathematics (not to speak of natural history) to suppose that these studies would be materially aided by ancient texts. In sum, Jefferson implicitly denied the classics any claim to a "real" matter.

Next, Jefferson asks: "To whom are these things useful? Certainly not to all men." They are to be acquired in early youth only. (It was, as I have mentioned, the pride of the humanists to sit down to Greek late in life.) The divine needs them in order to read both testaments, since the Septuagint is more accessible than the Hebrew Bible. The lawyer will be able to read our law at its Roman origins. The physician will at least find the "good Hippocrates" no worse that the "good Rush." The statesman can find there all sorts of subjects, even politics, if he supplements them with the modern science. Indeed, late in life Jefferson cited Aristotle and Cicero as the ancient sources of the Declaration of Independence (to Henry Lee, 8 May 1825), but I defy anyone to find a direct use. Finally, he thinks, all the sciences must go to the ancient languages for their etymological source. This turns out to be the most practical reason for their study, especially in view of the "neology" or word coinage Jefferson so enthusiastically advocated. However, Anglo-Saxon is more important in this respect. ("Rockfish Gap Report.")

The survey ends by excepting merchants and agriculturalists. These also need history, ethics, mathematics, and natural science, to be sure, but they do not need the ancient languages except for comfort and ornament. Which means: No one really *needs* them, neither the professional men nor those Homer-reading farmers.

I think I have shown that in Jefferson's personal love for the classical languages there lurks a pretty thorough repudiation. For all its enthusiasm, there is in it nothing of the essence and nothing publicly persuasive. It is a noble but baseless preference. It forebodes, despite his own convictions, the eventual loss of classical learning to American education in general, for it could certainly not be saved without a convincing claim that it contained worthwhile substance in irreplaceable language. The substantial and then the formal roots of this repudiation of the classics will be considered in the next section.

As for the other early republican writers, nearly all expressed themselves forcefully concerning this significant pedagogical matter. Tom Paine, as might be imagined, took a radical *tabula tasa* view: The books have all been translated; nothing new is to be learned from the dead languages; "the time expended on teaching and learning them is wasted." (*Age of Reason*, pt. 1.) He blamed the prevalence of "linguistry" on Christianity. He took issue with Jefferson's argument that there is a natural time when language learning is pedagogically suitable, and he claimed on the contrary that science learning and technical activity are appropriate to children.

There were, on the other hand, staunch classicists like the Marylander Samuel Knox, who shared with William Smith the prize awarded in 1797 by the American Philosophical Society for an essay on a national system of education. He argued along Jeffersonian lines, only more substantively, for the importance of classical languages to a knowledge of English.[33] Indeed, Jefferson is apt to have read the essay; in 1817 he unsuccessfully offered Knox the first university chair of languages (and any number of other subjects).

In between these extremes, there were the eminently reasonable reformers who ultimately prevailed even beyond their intentions, first and chief of whom was Benjamin Franklin. Their argument was not *against* classical learning but *for* English instruction. Franklin, in his "Proposals Relating to the Education of Youth in Pennsylvania" (1749), proposed something quite new for an actual school—the necessity of learning English first and by direct formal study, and the possibility of improving English style by reading English "classicks." Greek and Latin were to be elected by students in whom an "ardent desire" for them had been raised. It was the single pedagogical issue where Locke's influence was most direct and pervasive; in the serio-comic footnotes that stud the pamphlet, Franklin cited Locke's "Treatise on Education" and quoted it extensively.[34] It was a position so immediately sensible and appropriate to the situation that it was more and more often repeated, for example, by the physician Benjamin Rush and the lexicographer Noah Webster in their essays on republican education.[35] Franklin's work has no particularly destructive intention. Its first propagators were the most classically learned of Englishmen: Mulcaster in his *Elementarie*, and Milton, who in *Of Education* argued against a too early and too laborious "scraping together so much miserable Latin." But it had a devastating ultimate effect: Although all required the languages for the professions, all defended them as primarily ornamental—consequently, the modern wins over the ancient from sheer attention to making "men of business." The traditional learning needed leisure as the world required expedition. It should be added that by a kind of blessed inertia the colleges kept requiring Greek and Latin until the Civil War, when these finally yielded to the elective curriculum demanded by the proliferation of science.[36] I would conjecture that from that time the Republic showed a much lowered resistance with respect to its two great complementary linguistic afflictions: expert jargon and lay maundering.

All the Founders (among whom Paine, the exception, need not be numbered) had a classical training, some, especially Adams, Jefferson, and Madison, a very thorough one. They had the .taste and the tools to appropriate the classical tradition. They were founders of a polity without "a model on the face of the globe" (Madison, *Federalist* 14) who had the advantage of perfect self-awareness because they knew that which allowed them to distinguish the new from the old. Just one example: They knew in detail and from original sources what it was that made the antique participatory democracies unsuitable models for modern republics. (Madison, *Federalist* 10 and 14.) But they were in the condition of all successful liberating generations—they made that obsolete which made them what they were.[37] The problem is that, as the process of obsolescence progressed, their own Founding would be obscured. For when the ancients become inaccessible, the moderns become unintelligible.

Things, not Words

> Learning does not consist, as the schools now make it consist, in the knowledge of languages, but in the knowledge of things to which language gives names. [Paine, *Age of Reason*, pt. I.]

An expedient was therefore offered, that, since words are only names for *things*, it would be more convenient for all men to carry about them such *things* as were necessary to express the particular business they are to discourse on. [Swift, *Gulliver's Travels* III, 5, "Laputa."]

Jefferson proclaimed that "the greatest service which can be rendered any country is to add a useful plant to its culture, especially a bread grain." (Note to *Autobiography*.) To be sure, he finally preferred his epitaph to cite political documents and institutions of learning.[38] Yet the saying is significant; Jefferson belonged to that Baconian school which thought less of metaphysics than of political philosophy, less of politics than of science, and less of mathematical science than of natural history, less of classification than of practical applications.[39]

His plan for his great foundation expressed these biases. The University of Virginia was to be founded on "a plan so broad and liberal and *modern* as to be worth patronizing with the public support." (To Joseph Priestley, the discoverer of oxygen, 18 January 1800.) The deeply radical general character of this plan was that it was no unitary *ratio studiorum* but a completely eclectic composition of various materials, "which are good *for us.*" (To Carr, 7 September 1814.) Specifically, the University was to offer a larger proportion of science than any other school in the country. It was a truly new departure from the colleges in subject matter and, in consequence, in pedagogic form. The integrated curriculum of the college plan was replaced by a table of professional chairs, *schools* or *departments* as Jefferson himself fatefully called them. (To Carr, 7 September 1814.) Such departmental organization prevailed nearly completely in American colleges and universities after the Civil War. To the students Jefferson intended the concomitant to be "uncontrolled choice": "letting everyone come and listen to whatever he thinks may improve the condition of his mind." Students were not to be held to one "prescribed course of reading" or prevented from "exclusive application to those branches only which are to qualify them for particular vocations." (To Ticknor, 16 July 1832.) Jefferson first conceived exactly that mixture of choice and vocationalism which finally became the respectable

American mode for higher education when Eliot set out an elective plan for Harvard in his Inaugural Address of 1869. Ticknor, a friend and correspondent of Jefferson, was deeply impressed by the professional freedom and dedication to research of the German universities, particularly his own, Goettingen, and had attempted similar innovations at Harvard in the twenties.[40] Neither his nor Jefferson's ideas took real root until after the Civil War and the opening of the great state universities; as has been pointed out, in these matters Jefferson was a prophet rather than a founder. So much the more significant are his ideas, the results of a sure sense for educational modernity.

Now, such departmental arrangements were not absolutely tied to science. For example, Mulcaster had argued already in the sixteenth century for special colleges of languages, mathematics, philosophy, and the professions, including even the significant novelty of a teacher *training college*, (his term: *Positions*, 41). Neither were they necessarily tied to research, since Jefferson intended his university to be a teaching institution. Each generation, by adding its own discoveries and "handing the mass down for successive and constant accumulation, must advance the knowledge and well-being of mankind, not *infinitely*, as some have said, but *indefinitely*, and to a term which no one can fix or foresee." ("Rockfish Gap Report.") In other words, transmission of knowledge was still the central business of the school, but it was entirely in the interests of advancement, and that occurred largely in the sciences. But what the whole complex of pedagogical innovations really expressed from its earliest appearance was the abandonment of the unity of an education centered on the rational, speaking human being and the transfer of attention to the inexhaustible multiplicity of an intelligible and exploitable world. This is what made Jefferson's university essentially *modern*.

Accordingly, most chairs were assigned modern matter. To the traditional university arts, namely, classical languages, mathematics, and philosophy, there were added modern languages, the newer mathematical branches, contemporary philosophy, and three chairs of science with fourteen subjects (but no particular emphasis on mathematical science). The traditional professional faculties of medicine, law, and theology showed one vital addition: government, for which Jefferson set the new canon of authors. And there was one resounding omission: theology. ("Rockfish Gap Report.")

The transformation of philosophy and the relegation of theology quite literally to the periphery—the sects were to be allowed to keep competing religious establishments on the edge of the campus, which would serve to "neutralize their prejudices" (to Cooper, 2 November 1822)—are the feature of central interest here.

Jefferson several times sought Adams's advice about the new university. Adams's wry answers were never exactly in earnest, but once he tossed off a few sentences of real, if mordant, instruction. Jefferson's disregard of the advice is an index of the radicalism of his modernity. Adams wrote:

> When You asked my Opinion of a University, it would have been easy to Advise Mathematicks, Experimental Phylosophy, Natural History, Chemistry and Astronomy, Geography and the Fine Arts, to the Exclusion of Ontology, Metaphysics and Theology. But knowing the eager Impatience of the human Mind to search into Eternity and Infinity, the first Cause and last End of Things I thought best to leave it, its Liberty to inquire till it is convinced as I have been these 50 Years that there is but one Being in the Universe who comprehends it; and our last Resource is Resignation. [2 March 1816.]

His correspondent chose not to leave the mind its liberty so to inquire.

Jefferson was much interested in the ramifications of the "tree of sciences," that is, in the new Baconian divisions of the intellectual world (to Priestly, 18 January 1800), and especially in a spirit of improving on the master in its pruning. "A glance over Bacon's *arbor scientiae* will show ... how many of his ramifications of science are now lopped off as nugatory." (To Cooper, 25 August 1814.) The obviation of old sciences was of course among the most revolutionary of educational enterprises. D'Alembert, in his "Preliminary Discourse" to Diderot's *Encyclopedia*, devoted great attention to this tree, for it allowed the philosopher a vantage point high above the labyrinth of learning. In particular he acknowledged Bacon as the father of his enterprise, but he corrected him for being too timid in not cutting out the "study of general being," that is, ontology, in favor of research into individual beings.

Jefferson was a subscriber to the *Encyclopedia* in behalf of the State of Virginia, and he was so avid a reader that it took a Council resolution to retrieve the volumes that had been delivered to him. He organized his library according to the Baconian division of the intellectual world, which was, however, really the Encyclopedic classification—for where Bacon in the *Advancement* listed the fields of History, Poetry, and Philosophy corresponding to the faculties of Memory, Imagination, and Reason, d'Alembert and Jefferson had History, Philosophy, and Fine Arts, a division that reflected a great enlargement of the importance of the productive arts. Similarly, Jefferson justified the placing of military and naval architecture under Pure Mathematics in his study plan, as he explained to Adams, by reference to d'Alembert's *arbor scientiae* (15 August 1820); again, it was an encroachment of the applied on the pure sciences.[41]

The branch "lopped off," then, in this new university was that of divinity. The ostensible legal reason for so radical an omission was that it is unconstitutional for a state university to have a theological chair, since it must of necessity be sectarian.[42] But the intellectual and more fundamental cause was signified in the fact that the "proofs of the being of God . . . the author of all relations of morality" were assigned to the province of ethics (one of the five subjects, including *belles lettres* and fine arts, heaped on the professor of philosophy). That is to say, theology, once the queen science, was now a derivative, secondary subject. Moreover, as has been shown, ethics itself was not a very important study. Neither God nor the good were, then, intended to be intellectual preoccupations of the first republican university. It was a lack with a fateful immediate consequence, for in reaction to the "enlightened" removal of religion from the realm of public education there sprang up in the decades after the Revolution a profusion of small sectarian colleges.[43] They were usually poor and provincial, but they represented a popular and therefore perennial solution of a deep difficulty: "If it be easy to see that it is more particularly important in democratic ages that spiritual opinions should prevail, it is not easy to say by what means those who govern democratic nations may make them predominate." (Tocqueville, *Democracy in America*, II, bk. II, xv.) The coda to the development instituted by Jefferson in the universities is that toward the end of the nineteenth century the dignity of the divinity school had palpably passed to the business schools, "the perfect flower of the secularization of the universities." (Veblen, *The Higher Learning in America*, ch. 7.)

Nor was metaphysics admitted in Jefferson's school, in accordance with du Pont de Nemours's plan for the national university, which was to exclude the "unintelligible theological gibberish called *metaphysics*."[44] In the exact place that was traditionally assigned to First Philosophy, that is, to ontology or the science of being, Jefferson placed Ideology, the science of mind (and a word with a terrific future). Jefferson's Ideology was a doctrine, already mentioned in my first chapter, propagated by Destutt de Tracy, whom he considered with Dugald Stuart as "the ablest Metaphysician living; by which I mean Investigators of the thinking faculty of man." (To Adams, 14 March 1820.) His works "will render more service to our country than the writings of all the saints and holy Fathers of the church have rendered." (To Lafayette, 8 March 1819.) To make Ideology accessible in America, Jefferson himself corrected the translation of his "Treatise on Political Economy," which is prefaced by an outline of the doctrine of Ideology: Ideology is above all an antimetaphysical polemic, which leads to an empirical method of analysis. It begins in a critique of the human faculties in which they all come to be regarded as senses. An interaction between these and external matter is posited. The doctrine fitted well with Jefferson's "habitual anodyne," the transformed Cartesian formula, "I feel; therefore I exist." (To Adams, 15 August 1820.) This sensational materialism was also summed up in the fact that Tracy ranked it, and Jefferson accepted it, as a branch of zoology!—Jefferson's First Philosophy comes, strictly, under natural history.[45]

As far as the other republican writers are concerned, I believe

that not one proposed a return to *philological* as against *real*
subjects. A unique pre-Revolution college utopia, *The College of
Mirania*, written by the future provost of Franklin's College of
Pennsylvania, William Smith, set the tone. There were indeed
to be philosophical readings—Plato, Locke, and ethical works,
for the fifteen-year-olds. But the senior class was to be taught
Agriculture by the principal (whose name was *Aratus*, or *Cul-
tivator*)—the significance of this assignment lay in the fact that
traditionally the principal took the seniors for Moral Science. As
ever, actual practice was behind; Smith's program for the Philadelphia College culminated respectably in philosophical and
theological readings.[46] But the bitterest attack on philosophy
was made by Samuel Harrison Smith in the essay that in 1797
shared the prize of the Philosophical Society with Knox's. He
wrote that "philosophy withdraws the mind from useful employment by occupying it with considerations of idle curiosity";
it is an occupation "either unintelligible or uninteresting to
the young mind, while it delights in examining external appearances." However, again, remarkably, the most reputable
colleges continued to exercise their seniors in the traditional
scholastic metaphysical disputations until well after the Revolution;[47] indeed, it is among the more wonderful and significant
dispensations of the history of education how tenacious of life the
classical curriculum was in an ostensibly utilitarian country.
Nevertheless, the typical substance of American education was
to be *real*, as the "lopping off" became more ruthless; Justin
Morrill, later the sponsor of the Land Grant Law, which gave the
state universities their impetus, suggested in 1848 that American
colleges might well "lop off a portion of the studies established
centuries ago as a mark of European scholarship and replace the
vacancy—if it is a vacancy—by those of a less antique and more
practical value." The sequel, as is well known, is somewhat sad.
"Having stepped in Greek's vacated place, Science now occupies
its position, not with respect to size of enrollment, but with
respect to educational attitude. It is now in power and acts
disdainful, holier-than-thou, and prudish." And so science is
learnt by what is probably an even smaller proportion of the
population than once studied the classics.[48]

The last end of higher education for youths which Jefferson enunciates in the "Rockfish Gap Report" is "to form them to habits of reflection and correct action, rendering them examples of virtue to others, and of happiness within themselves." The question is whether the preferred public "real" curricula of a modern republic can by their very nature ever embody Jefferson's intention, quite apart from realizing his end. Republics, I have argued, are congenitally concerned with the realm of things and so with the world and its fruits, and Jefferson's materialist university is almost elegantly appropriate to a commonwealth. However, a connoisseur of democracy argues: "Materialism, among all nations, is a dangerous disease of the human mind; but it is more especially to be dreaded among a democratic people because it readily amalgamates with that vice which is most familiar to the heart under such circumstances. Democracy encourages a taste for physical gratification." (Tocqueville, *Democracy in America*, II, bk. 2, xv.)

In other words, the vigorous intellectual materialism that naturally forms part of the founding philosophy of this Republic (as will be further argued in the last chapter) will make a debilitating alliance with democratic tastes. Hence, this question becomes urgent: With the study of human and divine matters relegated to parochial education, does the public, or even the whole secular, realm of education eventually become incapable of forming those habits of reflection and that virtue which are peculiarly necessary to republics? The resolution of the dilemma would consist of reintroducing the roots of reflection and action into a recognizably republican curriculum.

Respect for Texts

Nothing seems to me more significant for the forming of the textual tradition in this country than Jefferson's own mode of reading. I begin with three tone-setting passages. Jefferson is apt to have seen only the last of them, but they catch perfectly the new spirit of repudiation of the authors' authority in education.

Montaigne advises the tutor to allow the pupil to "lodge nothing in his head on mere authority or trust," to imbibe Xenophanes' and Plato's ways of thinking, not their precepts.

"And let him boldly forget, if he wants, where he got them, and let him learn how to make them his own." (*Of the Education of Children.*) This was most precisely Jefferson's way. He had, out of extensive and persistent study in youth,[49] assimilated many views and phrases whose precise origin and context were no longer present to him. Indeed, the Declaration of Independence is a pastiche of the "harmonising sentiments of the day," reproduced without particular thought of their source and melded into "an expression of the American mind." (To Henry Lee, 8 May 1825.)

Again, in Locke's posthumous *Conduct of the Understanding* (20) the "true key of books and the clue to lead them through the mismaze of variety of opinions" is given to readers: Train yourself so that you can with "one cast of the eye, take a view of the argument and presently in most cases see where it bottoms." Here is a veritable incitement to feckless reading, which does not even concede with Bacon that some few books, at least, are "to be chewed and digested." (*Of Studies.*) And finally, Jefferson's youthful love, Bolingbroke, in a section on the use of texts, cites Boileau on translation: "tilt at the original . . . catch the spirit." (*Letters on the Study and Use of History*, No. 3.)

This is indeed the way in which Jefferson so industriously applied himself to texts. It was a labor carried on with an ever-fresh taste for learning, indomitable self-reliance of judgment, and an unclouded expectation that study aids action. But there are a host of dangers in it. For one thing it leads to hasty and hence uncontrolled colored interpretations. Such reading, even if it were not impermissible on the general ground of intellectual fidelity, would certainly be so in a Founder whose interpretations have weighty consequences.

Jefferson's expressions were measured on all matters but one: his virulent anticlericalism. It may have had personal sources and is not otherwise very edifying,[50] except that his reading of one ancient author, at least, was simply an adjunct to his aversion: Jefferson once reported to Adams (5 July 1814) an amazing activity: "I amused myself with reading seriously Plato's republic." He waded through the "whimsies" of this "soi-disant Christian" and concluded that the world consented to give reputation to such nonsense only because these whimsies were incorporated into the body of "artificial Christianity." His several references to Plato's "whimsies" were evidently lifted from the rabidly anticlerical Bolingbroke (as were also the comparisons of philosophers and Christians cited above). The attack on Plato as the father of priests and parsons, presumably through Neoplatonic Christianity, is a kind of Enlightenment tic;[51] it had apparently completely eclipsed the text for Jefferson.

He might have attacked Plato's *Republic* from the point of view of a practical American statesman, in the vein of Samuel Harrison Smith quoting Bacon's *Advancement*: "As for the philosophers, they make imaginary laws for imaginary commonwealths, and their discoveries are as the stars, which give little light, because they are so high."[52] Again, he might, with doubtful justice but some color of reason, have condemned Plato as an antidemocrat. Instead, he faulted his "foggy mind" simultaneously with his consummate sophistry, as well as his raw "Platonic republicanism," which would have us all living "pell-mell together, like beasts of the field or forest." In other words, he found what he cleverly called Plato's doctrine of "semblances" (that is, the *eidē*, "ideas," "forms," or "aspects"), which "can be defined neither in form or dimension," incomprehensible, while taking a crudely literal view of Socrates' commentary on the paranatural requirements of political community (in which Adams joined, 3 December 1813); he could make nothing of either his philosophy or his politics. But what he blamed Plato for principally was his having saved himself from early oblivion by providing the coming Christian priesthood with a mysticism more sophisticated than the simple doctrines of Christ, enabling them to "build up an artificial system which might, in its indistinctness, admit everlasting controversy," etc. His letter to Adams displays a curiously frivolous repudiation of the founder of political philosophy by a founder of American republicanism, especially astonishing if one considers that three key points in Jefferson's educational plan were anticipated in Plato's *Republic*: the necessity for setting up an advancing course of liberal learning for those fittest to govern by reason of their native genius and virtue; the distinction between the freedom of the "mass" of citizens to pursue their own business and the self-denying public service demanded of those set to guard the public happiness; and the unabashed project of revising scripture in the interests of virtue! It would perhaps be better not to read at all than to read so heedlessly.

A smiliar ascription of bad faith led to a somewhat reckless revisionism. In respect to Plato: "In truth his dialogues are libels on Socrates," whose name he used "to cover the whimsies of his own brain." And as he rescued Socrates from Plato, so he saved Jesus from the Gospel writers and Church Fathers and, again, the sophistications, perversions, and engraftings of that "Grecian sophist." (To Rush, 21 April 1803.) In fact, while president, Jefferson compiled a "Life and Morals of Jesus of Nazareth," the so-called Jefferson Bible, containing all the "genuine" parts of the Gospels stripped of their "inferior" theological accretions—that is, of all references to Jesus' divinity.[53] As was noted, the postponement of Bible study was intended precisely to encourage such criticism.

This confident critique, which disposes with equal facility of the delicate relation between Plato and his book-less teacher Socrates and of the mystery of the Incarnation, clearly had political implications. John Marshall, writing on the morning of Jefferson's first inauguration, classed him, in a division of Democrats into "speculative theorists" and "absolute terrorists," among the former—justly, for it is Jefferson's glory that his Enlightenment, as distinct from the French strain, did not issue in a Terror. Yet, the operative phrase is only a little less derogatory. It seems to me to be an expression of the new Chief Justice's distrust of a new President whose specific political ideas derived too much from an insufficient sense of the sacredness of founding scripture, from a certain cerebal recklessness such as on other occasions caused even the tactful Madison to intervene.[54]

For Jefferson, having decanonized the religious books, proposed to institute his own new political canon. The libertarian dilemmas of this intention with respect to citizen training have been noted. In the present context it is significant that in a realm where Jefferson was really engaged, that is, in the preparation of republican rulers, certain books were to have authority, to be the "text-books ... prescribed as the norma docendi," the teaching standard, by the authority of the trustees. (To Madison, 1 February 1825.) The new science of government was to be founded largely on American texts, for "I see with pride that we are ahead of Europe in Political science." (To Adams, 19 January 1819.) The required texts were, once again, to be: Locke's *Essay on Government*, Sidney, the Declaration of Independence, the Federalist, the Virginia Resolutions on the Alien and Sedition Laws, and Washington's Valedictory Address. Madison replied, gently, with some objections, first to the factional Republican element of the list (particularly the Virginia Resolutions, expressing a first formulation of the "states's rights" theory), but chiefly on the ground that these were not the texts to teach students to guard against "constructive violation" of republican charters, that is, against effective misinterpretation of the Constitution (8 February 1825), the absent item.

One indicative addendum: As Jefferson treated the older texts without piety, so did he the language itself: "I am a friend to *neology*.... What a language has the French become since the date of their revolution, by the free introduction of new words!" Then he cites, among others, *oxygen*, *electricity*, *centrality*, and *location*, and advocates—with humor somewhat outbalanced by enthusiasm—*neologist*, *neologisation*, *neologistical*, and five derivatives more. (To Adams, 15 August 1820.) I would argue that this untroubled repudiation of the sanctity of grown language, a natural consequence of a depreciation of the word, is the most pregnant of Jefferson's premonitions. An example: Jefferson, as previous citations bear witness, was, at least incidentally, concerned with the proper description of the noble calling of a republican legislator; after the fruition of his neologic revolution a similar preoccupation could be phrased in this manner: "The role of the legislator was conceptualized in terms of conflicts between internal and external variables and between role and idiosyncratic variables ... the socialization of legislators ... into their roles ... and the relevance of goals in different issue-areas as a source of differential behavior on the part of the same actors was explored." The precise English rendition of *neology* is *newspeak*. (Orwell, *Nineteen Eighty-four*, Appendix.)

In the other republican writers the energetic disrespect for the written word took a different and, from an educational point of view, even more consequence-laden turn. All of them—Jefferson, of course, at their head—called for the *diffusion* of knowledge. They understood that such diffusion requires its own intellectual and institutional conditions: a methodical knowledge that can be widely and expeditiously imparted, foundations for its orderly generation, and a system of institutions for its propagation. I referred in the first chapter to their call for a national university, that is, for a central institution supervising a system of national education.[55]

Now, the most necessary teaching tool for a republican diffusion of knowledge was seen by them to be the textbook. Thus, Samuel Knox has a whole chapter "On the Advantages of Introducing the Same Uniform System of Schoolbooks into a Plan of Public Education." By a *textbook*, as opposed to a *text*, I mean manuals of prepared, convenient teaching material written in conventional technical language. Textbooks, then, are opposed to works that are original in both senses of the term, in being the discoveries or reflection of the writer himself, and in taking a study to its intellectual origins, using the original language of discovery. In sum, textbooks follow primarily a scheme of presentation; texts convey the order of inquiry.

Since textbooks are the natural adjunct to a centralized system of education, naturally the French writers of the Enlightenment were most insistent on their use. La Chalotais, Turgot, Diderot, Condorcet—all prescribed textbook-making as the beginning of educational reform.[56] The *Encyclopedia* itself is the spirit of textbook-writing incarnate: d'Alembert happily condoned "the multiplication of 'methods', of 'elements', of 'abridgements', and of 'libraries'." ("Preliminary Discourse," pt. III, beginning.)

Of course, textbooks were nothing new; digests, doctrinals, compendia were inflicted on medieval students. But with

Comenius, who called for books specially composed for his classes (*Great Didactic* 33), textbook-making became a deliberate and massive pedagogical activity. And this innocuous-seeming enterprise turned out to be the most insidiously potent of all the repudiations of the textual tradition, for it abolished that trusting expectation of inexhaustible meaning which a reader is entitled to bring to an original text. Textbook dogma drives out textual authority—here is the fundamental revolution on the formal side of education, that is, in the form in which studies come to the student.

Without positively deciding which was ultimately cause and which consequence—the approach to the textual tradition or the social disposition that fit it—it is observable that modes of study have wide political implications. Reverence is a universal educational problem. The imaginative incarnation of this general human truth is Goethe's pedagogical province in *Wilhelm Meister, Journeyman* (II, 1). Here, just because it is devoted to the full development of the children's humanity, the training begins with the inculcation of forms of reverence, which are in no way incompatible with high spirits. Madison, again, urges the special importance of a reverential disposition, in the form of "reverence for the law," to the stability of a free government, a phrase caught up by Lincoln, whose early speech on "The Perpetuation of Our Political Institutions" is preoccupied with the same political problem. But one might also argue that this sentiment is vitally necessary in a modern republic, not only for political stability but, even more acutely, for human serenity. The reason is that, in a setting where the person and his choices are infinitely valued and where there is no public realm of religion, the price of public irreverence is private nerves. Without some general gravity, individual dignity becomes very laborious. Yet a lack of gravity, and its accompaniment, an overstimulated boredom with any classical expression, is endemic to democracies, where the old imitate the young "so that they may not seem kill-joy authoritarians." (Plato, *Republic*, VIII, 563 b.) It shows itself crucially in an education that is intended, in Jefferson's words, "to enlarge and enlighten the mind of our youths." For this liberating function has solidity only when some degree of respectful attention precedes, as the case of the learned Founders themselves shows.[57] If, on the other hand, there is a reckless abrogation of the tradition, then liberation, lacking a "place where to stand," become an empty and self-consuming, hectic formalism. In a law-based, democratic republic, the fostering of scriptural reverence ought, therefore, to be an essential part of a properly republican education. A secular version of *credo ut intellegam*, something like "I trust, so that I may learn," is a necessary part of the devotions due to liberty.

In each of the three ways set out, the tradition is repudiated by Jefferson and the other early writers on education, repudiated in a knowledgeable, exemplary, and urbane way, in a way attuned to the polity that their educational views are meant to serve. It is a polity from its roots too busy in the shaping of the world for long initiations, in need of applicable and conveyable knowledge, impatient of authority. Thence comes a loss of that kind of access to the tradition which requires careful preparation, thence the displacement of *rational* by *real* knowledge, thence the audacious treatment of all manner of sacred and secular scripture. Yet this, or any, republic, whose very reason for being is the public good, depends on well-grounded, thoughtful, even wise, citizens. Is there a way to resolve this paradoxical relation, particularly of modern republican life to republican requirements, of devising education for this Republic that is careful, reflective, and respectful without being the less taut, substantial, and independent? I think there may be such a way, and it will be the recovery of the very tradition in which the Founders who repudiated it were so well versed.

ATTEMPTED RESOLUTION OF THE PARADOX OF TRADITION

I propose to give reasons and ways for saving the study of the Western tradition as the central means of education. I have circumscribed what I mean by education in the Introduction, namely, the literate activity of a leisured interlude between childhood and professional training. My undertaking is nothing if it cannot be sensible. By a sensible approach I mean one wittingly obtuse to mere current circumstances and very much alive to their roots. As I have urged, it is at its beginnings that our present condition becomes amenable to understanding and to fundamental alteration.

Now, that beginning is not only brave and exhilarating but deliberate and informed, and so its consequences have some happy marks: an enormous people largely literate, invincibly moderate, habitually principled, and ready to support a multifarious conglomerate of institutions that, at the least, make no kind of learning impossible. It is only sensible to suppose that our troubles display nothing but the vices of our virtues. And so, again, my last intention is to vilify our times or our institutions, our so-called educational system, which, happily, is no system at all. On the contrary, I can imagine no time or place that offers a more convenient conjunction of safety and opportunity, of protecting institutions and available devices for weasling through and turning to account all manner of apparently unavoidable nonsense to accomplish some local good.

So far, I have generally avoided the term *democratic* in favor of *republican*. The reason has been that, although this Republic is under a democracy, that is, under popular rule, the term *democratic*, partly through Tocqueville's influence, has come to mean less a polity than a configuration of social modes. Chief of these is egalitarianism, the desire for equality, not in certain definite respects to ensure certain definite possibilities, but as an absolute actualized good. It is its obverse term, *elitism*, that, as has been set out, frequently figures in educational considerations. But it seems to me to be among those very circumstantial issues which should be carefully overlooked, since it simply confuses the great question, "What should a citizen learn?" A premature regard for equality of distribution paralyzes educational reflection, which should make the universally desirable the eminently thinkable. Worries concerning inequality of talent seem to me gratuitous as well—as prodigious stupidity is much rarer than terrific cleverness, so the general intelligence is, I think, quite sufficient for genuine education. So I shall simply assume without further proof, axiomatically, in accordance with the Declaration of Independence, that there are certain matters of equal importance to all letter-nourished, Constitution-governed, science-dependent citizens. At the same time, it seems to me sensible to think that if a plan is good in itself, and therefore good for any two or twenty or two-hundred citizens, it is better for the whole Republic to make a small beginning with it than to deprecate the attempt because the other two hundred and twenty million are not immediate participants.

The Pedagogical Form

As for the ways for recovering the tradition, they come under three headings that I can see: *Time*, *Teaching*, and a *Study Plan*.

It is sensible to suppose that the *time* allotted for the formal education I propose should be clearly circumscribed and bracketed, as it were, for this purpose as an interlude of responsible leisure. For these, and for other reasons I have given, it should be a college plan. In order to make it generally accessible it should be so self-contained and self-sufficient as to rely as little as possible on a particular secondary school training. Training in the ancient languages is not an unthinkable requirement—it is eminently thinkable, since there has already been an occurrence when a whole learned world studied Greek in adulthood—but it is at this moment as absurd as it is unnecessary to make it a condition for beginning the course of education. Nor is an adequate "historical background" to be required or quickly administered. For one thing, it is an impractical undertaking. The kind of account that is intended to explain the genesis of texts would, were it in principle possible, need to be practically infinite—veracity and synopsis are by and large mutually incompatible in history, which is therefore only very crudely conveyable in outline.[58] For another, such an account stultifies the object. For how can a background explain the works of intellects precisely distinguished for their radical originality and spontaneity? The need for such preparation implies that the authors are both defenseless victims of their times and deficient in circumspection in their composition—when the virtues of independence and sufficiency were precisely the criteria of their selection.

The education I mean should require only moderate English literacy and elementary algebra. Those modest requirements will assure that this education is essentially elementary, that is to say, that it takes hold of studies in a way carefully devised to be a true beginning and not merely a starting point.

As far as *teaching* is concerned, it is a happy circumstance that the way most appropriate to what I propose is also the most republican, even democratic, of pedagogical modes. This way is often called Socratic—falsely, if the Socrates of the *Dialogues* is meant to be its model, for his conversations are artfully superintended by Plato, and all his questions are compellingly leading questions—but truly, if a certain frank and friendly intention to aid inquiry and to discourse free from reference to secondary opinion is meant. In this latter sense there is an indigenous American Socratism, expressed, for example, in the Trustees' pamphlet issued in behalf of the College of New Jersey in 1754. They

> have endeavour'd to improve, upon the commonly received Plan of Education. They proceed not so much in the Method of dogmatic Institution, by prolix Discourses , on the different Branches of the *Sciences*, by burdening the Memory, and imposing heavy and disagreeable Tasks; as in the *Socratic* Way of free Dialogue, between Teacher and Pupil, or between the Students themselves, under the Inspection of their Tutors. In this Manner, the Attention is engaged, the Mind entertain'd, and the Scholar animated in the Pursuit of Knowledge. In fine, the Arts and Sciences are convey'd into the Minds of Youth, in a Method, the most easy, natural, and familiar.[59]

As at Princeton for pedagogical reasons, so in Philadelphia for prudential purposes: Franklin, having read some Socratic dialogues "was charmed with the method for life . . . and put on the humble inquirer and doubter." (*Autobiography*, at age sixteen.) In his unpretentious dignity and purposeful openness, at least, Socrates is indeed the aboriginal American—and in his deeper aspects he *should be* naturalized.

The pedagogical problem can be seen in the light of the terms introduced earlier. It is to find a composition of the extremes of *transmission* of learning (with its paraphernalia of lectures, outline notes, quizzes, etc.), *advancement* (whose associated academic terms are research, or better, *"my* work," original contributions, etc.), and *diffusion* (that is, introductory courses, exposures, etc.).

Despite much lamentation, the opposition between transmission and advancement—with diffusion as a makeshift mean—has totally possessed institutions of higher learning. In America this condition is mostly the consequence of an early enthusiasm for and ultimate acceptance of the German university model. Wilhelm von Humboldt, who was Prussian Minister of Public Instruction in the early nineteenth century, described the university as an institution whose "isolation and freedom" is carefully protected, which is given to "investigation and research," thus considering all knowledge as a "not yet wholly solved problem," and which is emphatically not directly committed to education.[60] Newman, on the other hand, boldly asserted in the preface of *The Idea of a University* that a university "is a place of *teaching* universal *knowledge*" whose object is "the diffusion and extension of knowledge rather than the advancement," which latter is located in learned societies. Thus, while the institutional terms are different in England, the pedagogical split is the same.

These two separate enterprises are both good and necessary for something, but not for the education as such of citizens in a republic. For that, another mean is needed, which I shall term *inquiry*, an activity in which teaching and learning are not quite separable. It might be called Socratic if the *imitatio Socrati* were not a piece of temerity. It is devoid of any intention to add to the collectible store of information; it has no relation at all to the newness or oldness of knowledge, being altogether intent on thinking things anew rather than on thinking new things. Positively, it is an intention—much more dependent for its realization on desire than on talent, and therefore potentially universal—to be thoroughly aware of what one does and says and thinks. It becomes actual teaching insofar as the intention is skillfully converted into an orderly public process. Such teaching is a sort of wisdom in practice or a practical love of wisdom, whose chief requirement in point of character is a certain proud shamelessness. But it does not become more vivid with more words.

As for the *plan of studies*, taken from the point of view of its form, it must be, I am sorry to say, in some degree required. This, in turn, means that not all useful learning can be admitted into the scheme—which is, of course, precisely what makes it a plan. The "Yale Faculty Report" of 1828 made this point classically:

> But why, it is asked, should *all* the students in a college be required to tread in the *same steps*? Why should not each one be allowed to select those branches of study which are most to his taste, and which are most nearly connected with his intended profession? To this we answer that our prescribed course contains those subjects only which ought to be understood, as we think, by everyone who aims at a thorough education. They are not the peculiarities of any profession or art. . . . The collegiate course of study is far from embracing everything which the student will ever have occasion to learn. The object is not to finish: but to lay the foundation.[61]

On the other hand, those studies that are required must be offered with conviction and confidence, and then they will not be initially resisted. But once embarked on, they are even less likely to be rejected, for such rejection occurs "where the judge presumeth and knoweth not the skill, which he saith is naught. . . . I wish they had them, which mislike what they have not, and give ignorance the reign. For if they had them, we should hear no speech but praise and proof, admiration and honor." (Mulcaster, *Positions*, 41.) Hence, an argument about the relevance of an unread book is a pedagogical futility.

As far as the student's preference is concerned, the chief choice should be whether to be educated or not. As I have argued, it is only sensible to admit that, although a true education is essential to the best public life, in a republic as happily instituted as ours, an ordinary upbringing can produce a decent public tone, which might become corrupted under a forced system of higher education. But, once the choice is made, a certain reckless eagerness for truth in young students and a matured need in older learners can be relied on to make them accept a rigorous program that is perhaps not immediately and obviously relevant to their personal concerns. Besides, hardly enough can be made of the friendship to be found in the republic of letters and community of common studies. Joel Barlow was quite right: The liberal sciences are in their very nature republican; "they delight in reciprocal communication."

The Educational Means

I want to argue then, first, that not merely private taste, but public reasons, which slipped away in the time of the first repudiation, can be adduced for the study of the collection of texts, chiefly of poetry, science, and philosophy, that I have called *the tradition*. I shall take it as given that the core of this collection is fairly established among its devoted students and that the perennial argument about its periphery serves only to revivify a sense of its corporateness. The listing of these books is unavoidable pedagogically but absurd as a preoccupation. Second and more particularly, I want to propose that within the tradition are to be found exact studies that, while offering the best aids to inquiry in my sense, are also fundamental and necessary to mastering life in the Republic.

Let me go about fixing my ideas by using a Baconian form with a classical content. It is open to the objection of employing an antiquated "faculties psychology." But to me it seems quite adequate, and ultimately in these matters: "When I shall have set down my own reading orderly, and perspicuously, the pains left another, will be only to consider, if he also find not the same in himself. For this kind of doctrine admitteth no other demonstration." (Hobbes, *Leviathan*, Intro.)

Authors. The works of the tradition then seem to me to arise from these sources: from the imagination, an inner receptacle for internally produced and reproduced images of sight and sound; from the reason, a faculty for grasping and grouping things and arguments; and from the intellect, a capacity for thinking on thought itself, for reflection. To these faculties correspond first *poetry*, in English, "made" or fictional forms or contents in the widest sense; then rationally constructed knowledge of the world, the *science* of nature; and finally *philosophy*, accounts given, as the word signifies, of the fruits of the love of wisdom. It goes without saying that good poetry is also informed by the intellect, scientific constructs are initiated as well by the imagination, and philosophy is often completed in myth, and also that there are probably nonpractical human activities not comprehended in this scheme.

Now, scarcely anyone would argue that poetry is ever the more interesting because it is earlier—Jefferson hardly considered Homer best because he was first. Indeed, by the Socratic criterion that "the tragic poet of true art is also a comic poet" (*Symposium* 223 d), a certain Elizabethan poet surpasses any Greek. Nor is the old literary saw about reading Homer for the understanding of Virgil, Virgil for Dante, Dante for Milton very profitable—thus every poem becomes an ancilla. The poetic tradition is essentially truly timeless; the oldest and the most recent poets can be read pell-mell as well as in some improving order. (Clearly, what holds for the appreciation does not hold for the making of poetry, which is a craft very much in a temporal tradition.) All that is needed to make a poet accessible is a good translation—obviously, the Jeffersonian preference for originals must sadly but certainly be relinquished. Curiously enough, teachers discover that just in poetry, where the translations lose the most, they are least minded.

There is a certain temptation to recommend the classics of poetry and music and fine arts in a passion of melancholy ardor for our waning Western grandeur. But in spite, or rather because, of its truth, that sentiment had best be kept out of sight. In any case, in respect to the poetic tradition an exchange of pedagogic ways and means is much more needful than an argument for its importance. For instance, it is a question to what extent the training of the sensibility should be a severely intellectual discipline and to what extent more an appreciative consideration. But however poetry is studied, it is vitally necessary to us. For the pedestrian and private pursuit of happiness for which this Republic was explicitly founded begs to be complemented by common cultivation and sources of levitating delight. No polity is more in need of model images to give resonance to inner life and reference to the public scenes. And that is what poetry provides.

Next is the study of science. Few people disagree that the study of nature is, on the other hand, progressive, that it proceeds by superseding and converting former systems into special cases. That fact makes especially pertinent the question why the early founding works of the tradition should be imposed on students, why the streamlined, sophisticated contemporary treatments of the same matter would not be pedagogically more expeditious and gain time for pushing on. Now, where the object is to make the student a professional scientist, to enable him to be in the "forefront" and to try for "breakthroughs" (for here there really are such), there the most sophisticated teaching by the most advanced scientist is no doubt best. But all citizens do not expect to further science; they expect to live with it and its works. This potent enterprise would be intellectually fascinating merely because it has succeeded in arrogating to itself the name of *knowledge* (*scientia*); it is, furthermore, full of beautiful objects and elegant theories that it is a pity and a shame to ignore. Above all, however, a knowledge of the knowledge, that is to say, of the *science* of nature is indispensable to self-knowledge: because nature does still contain us, because through her science this environment is altered, because the study of nature is a central human mode— but most of all, because there exists a nonnegligible claim that nature is *our* projection and *our* construct. It follows that science is a humanly necessary constituent of education, so long as it is science not professionally but reflectively studied.

Now, that is not in principle impossible from fine textbooks and gifted scientists. But for some reason—mostly because of their bright and ambitious impatience—it rarely takes place. Let me give an example of what I mean by the reflective study of science, and the unlikelihood of its occurring even in an elementary science course will be patent. I open four reputable textbooks in elementary physics. Each uses, from the very beginning, the first dimensionally secondary quantity of the science of motion, namely, velocity. (By a dimensionally secondary quantity is meant one compounded of the elementary quantities, as velocity, S/T, is compounded of space, S, and time, T.) Thus I observe that all four books begin past the point where naive questions might be asked. Yet who understands without reflection how the time, how the place in which we live and have our being, can be transmogrified into mere magnitudes capable of entering into a ratio, and how those magnitudes have in turn been transformed into quantities able to constitute a rational number? All such questions are regarded in textbooks as outside of actual physics. And yet they can never be considered with any immediacy in the abstracted fields of philosophy of science or history of science, but only in the actual context of real if elementary science. But considered they must be, for our problematic modernity is the residue of such transformations.

To put it more broadly: It is absolutely necessary for a citizen of this Republic to understand at least in an elementary way how nature is prepared to become the object of science, both pure and applied. It is necessary to consider the process by which the world is turned from a place into an "environment," and nature from a source into a "resource." Such transformations are not wicked impositions but the phenomenal concomitants of a radically new mode of being in the world—technology—whose intellectual principle is science. And since such issues always were and are now universally understood to be political, the argument is complete.

Similarly, it is necessary to reflect on the bearing of science on the reinterpretation of human matters. Our language displays us as "contacting" each other, having "interactions" with one another, as engaging in "dynamic" relationships. This is the language of the physics of moving bodies, and those who use it should understand what they are saying.

Now, I am arguing that for us it is to be either tradition or technique, that we either return to the roots or fall prey to the consequences. The argument is at first mainly pedagogic. The first discoverers of modern science were still open to naive fundamental questions. For example, in that founding work of physics, *The Dialogues Concerning Two New Sciences*, Galileo devotes a small treatise to the establishment of the same quantity of velocity (or rather, speed), I mentioned above.[62] The study of this work (of course accompanied by suitable laboratory work) is consequently not so much an indispensable as a practical way into the matter—not to speak of the fact that Galileo is the most charming of scientific writers. Naturally, students must be prepared at least with that elementary kind of mathematics Galileo himself knew. Happily, these preparatory works, above all Euclid's *Elements*, are not mere compendia of propositions and techniques; they are themselves great vehicles of reflection; as I mentioned in my first chapter, it used to be understood that mathematics of this kind was the necessary prelude to philosophy: "Let no one ungeometrical enter here" was said to be the inscription on the gate of Plato's Academy.[63] And, once students are ready for them, the works of Galileo and Kepler and Newton do more to dispel that artificial difficulty, termed with inspired infelicity "the two cultures,"[64] than all the clever physics-for-dolts courses devisable.

These straightforward and sensible reasons for reading sources can be grounded in a subtle philosophical theory. It can be argued that sources are not only pedagogically convenient but philosophically necessary, precisely because of the progressive character of science. In each of its superseding movements the scientific enterprise enters a higher state of abstraction and becomes more remote from and forgetful of its immediately intelligible origins; there is a *sedimentation* of significance.[65] It is obvious that this source study is only most accidentally "history of science," since the point is not to describe accurately the circumstances and works of the past but to recover inner meanings properly belonging to the present.

If works of poetry are essentially timeless, while the discoveries of science are made, in Newton's phrase, by "standing on the shoulders of giants,"[66] philosophical works are related in both and neither fashion. Almost all such works address their predecessors, who cannot, being dead, reply pointedly in turn but whose case is revived by their opponents' successors. Hence, the philosophical tradition proceeds, but not progressively; it is rather a kind of spiral on which the motion comes periodically over the same position, but at a higher level. When I say higher

I mean, however, an extremely dubious and problematic rise, which may, in truth, be a fall. For it may be unavoidably the case that "in arts mechanical the first deviser comes shortest, and time addeth and perfecteth; but in sciences [that is, philosophy; Plato and Aristotle are among those instanced] the first author goeth farthest, and time leeseth and corrupteth." (*Advancement*, I, iv, 12.) It is at least possible that in philosophy all successors are unavoidably epigones and their works attenuating elaborations and leveling explications of the original deep insight. The possibility must be contemplated that in philosophy a pejorative principle is at work, that the loss of innocence, of immediacy, of naiveté, must in the very nature of the thing bring with it a loss of depth. Such a sophisticated loss may characterize not only ordinary development but even those radical and abrupt reinterpretations which mark the epochs of the philosophical tradition, above all that abysmal breach between the ancients and the moderns of which this Republic is the political incarnation. The question whether philosophy, too, is an advancing or a decaying, a culminating or a cyclical enterprise is itself one of the burning modern issues. However, it should be noted that at least one philosopher, who certainly considered it progressive, did not thereby consider himself released from the study of the tradition: "The safest general characterization of the European philosophical tradition is that it consists of a series of footnotes to Plato." (Whitehead, *Process and Reality*, II, i, 1.)

What is more, the tradition should be taken up at first hand. One argument against secondary presentation lies in the inconclusiveness of the tradition: "Knowledge that is delivered as a thread to be spun on, ought to be delivered and intimated, if it were possible, in the same method wherein it was invented." (*Advancement*, II, xvii, 4, "Method of Tradition.") That is to say, it is next to impossible to think on from a textbook. In general, it is only reasonable to suppose that a writer capable of deep inquiry is capable of finding those terms and that format which are inseparable from his meaning, so that to put it otherwise is to put another thing; to attempt to convey one author's meaning in a successor's terms is to corrupt his sense;

only the original context can mitigate the sometimes unavoidable sins of translation. Besides, students are much more apt to suspend disbelief long enough to think when confronted with an original if perplexing text, than if they are presented, by someone "teaching Plato," with some remote and unlikely hearsay about his "believing" in "forms," and other unintelligibilia. Students have even felt impelled to study the original languages as a result of such a tempting and troubling encounter.

But all this is not yet reason why a citizen should read philosophy, especially when the indigenous mode of the Republic is said to be pragmatism. Now, when that judgment is merely a form of Buffon's old argument (for the strenuous rebuttal of which Jefferson wrote his *Notes on Virginia*) that human nature degenerates on this continent, it "does not deserve the compliment of rational opposition." If, again, it means that Americans peculiarly prefer the sophisticated philosophical views called pragmatism, then it is implied that they do philosophize, and very acutely at that, since a pragmatist must trace all his notions through practice to test their truth. But if it implies that, beginning with their Founders, they are apt to listen to "the voice of reasonableness not Reason,"[67] then the case for a philosophic education is indeed well and truly made. For that is the precise description of a felicitously prephilosophical state: The living fabric of this country is shot through with reasonings (of which more in the chapter on Rationality); its documents refer to truths we hold to be self-evident and propositions to which the nation is dedicated. But wherever reason is at work in the world as reasonableness, there reflection is both especially at home and especially called for. I note here also a circumstance to be taken up in the last chapter, that philosophy is centrally concerned with what is common and public in the most essential sense, and so with the very exemplar in thought of a republic.

The best reason, however, for reading the philosophers is, at least in the first instance, suprapolitical. One may argue that the love of wisdom is the mark of human excellence, *par excellence*. In ancient cities, which lived by tradition in the widest sense, philosophizing was regarded by some as a deeply suspect, and by others as the noblest, activity, but, by those who knew it best, as both at once. However, just because it was an excellence, it was not a common requirement. I would argue that we moderns require it precisely as moderns, just because our life is informed by rational constructs, immaterial and material, by theories, techniques, instruments, and machines. Each of these, being a creation of rationality, addresses itself to our reason, which, without the perspective of the philosophical tradition, is readily stunned into an uneasy illusion of familiarity. Nothing so subtly distracts human beings as an environment of vestigially thoughtful speech and uninterpretable objects of reason emitting a persistent rational gibberish. The great philosophical works that created this diffuse juggernaut are also the means of turning our compacted confusion into that attentive estrangement Socrates used to call *wondering*: "for to wonder—that is the special affection of a philosopher." (*Theaetetus* 155 d.) What was an exemplary culmination for the ancients is for us a common necessity. That is, after all, the measure of our advance.

There is no denying that the ways of study here advocated embody the rudiments of a philosophical determination[68]—as does, willingly or unwillingly, every plan of education or training. Any course of reading requires, to put it loftily, a *hermeneutic*, an interpretative scheme.[69] *This* scheme is the positive complement to the rejection of a historical study of the tradition. Such study, I have argued, begs all the questions, for if the text assumes, as do most major works, a radical originating power of thought, then to offer to explicate it by providing its historical setting is simply to deny the truth of the text before making it read. I dismiss, on the basis of experience, the pedagogical contention that students cannot read books without such preparation, which is largely a way of saying that the teacher does not believe in their intelligibility.

The positive prejudgment, then, is precisely this: that each text is to be approached as if it might contain truth; the students are asked to ask themselves whether what they are reading is *true*. But by stipulating this much, I have called up, in its most acute form, the ever-unresolved dilemma of writings on education, which is, that even the most innocuous pedagogical plan involves deep, if tacit, assumptions. Thus to tell just what is behind this potent principle of reading, which certainly runs counter to the conventions of the academy, is the same as to present the interpretation of certain philosophical books, since much of the tradition is preoccupied with finding its own conditions of possibility. Without tapping substance beyond the occasion, I can at least say that one working assumption seems to me most necessary and most binding: that there *is* rational speech, *logos*.

I should add that this high demand of possible truth does not mean that sometimes books of admittedly less stature should not be studied. There are certain concededly shoddy books that circumstances have made overwhelmingly influential. These, too, may be read seriously and in good faith; but they will provide insight into prevailing opinion rather than into the nature of things. It is an important political duty to read them—but not only them.

And finally there are certain books that confirm the sharp definition of the interpretative principle precisely as they reject it. These are mostly books of recent modernity that incorporate the claim that the early childhood of human beings ultimately shapes the thoughts of their maturity or that economic origins determine their most vital opinions. If these texts are read by their own criteria, they cannot, by their own thesis, tell truth in any established sense; if they are read by the principle here proposed, they are by that very circumstance convicted of having claimed what is false. I make this point only for the sake of candor, to display the fact that the proposed principle of reading, not being a mere formalism, is in some sense exclusionary. Yet, even so, it at least requires *all* texts to be taken immediately and seriously. As a working rule it is, after all, more pedagogical than philosophical.

Arts. I have made an argument for the great authors; now let me make, briefly but with only slightly less conviction, an argument for that complementary aspect of the tradition, the free arts.

The best way to show that they ought to be the preferred propaedeutic to reflection is to distinguish them from other modes of categorizing learning matter.

The liberal *arts* are essentially ancillary to knowledge. According to medieval authors, the arts "bind" (*artant*) with rules of great "virtue" (*aretē*).[70] The etymologies are idle, but the sense is not; the arts consist of rules with their reasons, examples, exceptions, exercises—but matter only incidentally. The rules and procedures of the arts are time-tried and arranged according to pedagogical experience, often even in preference to the order of their inner logic. Thus, the arts induce skills of inquiry while authors convey propositions of knowledge. For example, that famous "Asses' Bridge," the fifth proposition of Euclid's *Elements*,[71] that "in isosceles triangles the angles at the base are equal to one another," is a proposition, to be sure, but it is not for the sake of its truth that the proof is studied (since that is seen immediately), but in order to learn to distinguish certain intellectual objects and to exercise the rule-bound reason on them. (It is almost comically indicative that the Asses' Bridge—the *fifth* proposition of plane geometry—was the downfall of Vico's mathematical studies, *Autobiography* [1725]; Vico was a founder of modern historiography and, as has been mentioned, an early proponent of the humanities in opposition to natural science.) The parallel array of arts and authors is pedagogically useful for a reflection on the difference between *knowing how* and *thinking that*.

It must be observed here that arts can yield *methods* when they are applied with purpose and philosophical justification to a certain realm, as mathematics may be applied to nature, logic to deliberation, and music, for example, to therapy. Again, one or the other may be generalized into a "universal art," as Descartes did with mathematics to found the "analytic method." (*Rules for the Direction of the Mind*, Rule 4, on the analytic method.) It follows that, as is often suggested, to teach students *methods of analysis* as if they were neutral intellectual tools is insidiously to indoctrinate them, and very powerfully, too. In any case, both arts and methods are perfectly incapable of teaching students to think; indeed, you can teach people to think as soon as you can teach them to be. It is only a question of directing their inborn desire to know; a student can be "taught *how* to learn." ("Yale Report" of 1828.)

Again distinguishable from either arts or authors as a categorization of knowledge are *fields*. They are the concomitant of the advancement of learning: Bacon's *Instauratio Magna* contains a catalogue of proposed histories, each the textbook of a future field of specialized knowledge, as for example, a history of pottery—the typical monograph of as modern a field as any, archaeology. Fields employ methods and are founded on those intellectual decisions called theories. They also have a criterion of respectability: objectivity. The limitless plane of modern knowledge was leveled for division into fields by a genuinely revolutionary upheaval, a truly enormous intellectual shifting. The way of inquiry (*methodos*) had to be turned into *method*, contemplation (*theoria*) into *theory*, being and appearance into *subject* and *object*. Students come to college at least acquainted with some fields of knowledge. For the sake of knowing their own knowledge, they should be granted a time of enforced inchoateness before they go on to advanced study in the field they choose. This is precisely where the reading of the originating authors assures the greatest freedom from presuppositions: *their* subject matter is not yet firmly fenced in; the divisions of knowledge are still in question. And the arts, insofar as they are skills rather than contents, leave the intellectual world similarly indeterminate. Such a preparation seems to me of supreme importance, especially to those students who choose the social studies (those bastard births by science out of political theory), which are so fascinating and influential to the citizens of modern republics. They are far too problematic to be a proper undergraduate study.

Again, within the arts themselves there occurs that fateful division that is so indispensable to reflection on our academic condition. It is the distinction, mentioned before, between the arts of significant speech and the arts of intelligible things. To recapitulate: the *trivium* consists traditionally of the art of reading or "grammar," that is, literature; of the art of persuasive speaking or "rhetoric" (as we would say, "communications"); and of "logic," the art of the binding connections of speech, formal language. The *quadrivium* consists of the mathematical or "learnable" arts, so called because they concern intelligible objects, which are traditionally ordered according to increasing corporeality, from dimensionless arithmetic through plane and solid geometry, to astronomy (the application of mathematics to moving bodies) and music (the study of bodies executing harmonious motions, that is, physics). (*Republic* VII, 525 ff.)

I am recapitulating the traditional arts scheme only to argue that, when concretely realized in a classroom, it has a certain peculiar pedagogical value. It encourages students to regard language and mathematics as originally related, equally accessible, and perfectly compatible human skills. (And incidentally, it provides a reflective setting for some of that additional training in both which most students need.) At the same time it invites discussion of their differences and of the origin and reason for the modern gulf between the humanities and the sciences.

Finally, it would be absurd to claim that the arts, elementary as they are intended to be, are sufficient to give competence in any branch of modern knowledge. But then, I have heard of no plan of education that is; the more anxiously comprehensive, the more embarrassing most such programs are. Competence is a matter for graduate, professional, and technical schools. The liberal arts scheme, on the other hand, has a time-tried integrity—it is at least arguable that language and mathematics are in fact the two root activities of the human understanding—while, just because they are root skills, they are always applicable to new matter. A faculty forgoing fields and departments in favor of the arts will not be doing what is sufficient but, perhaps, what is necessary.

Rationality

3

"Philosophical Method of the Americans" is the startling chapter heading with which Tocqueville begins his disquisition on American civil society:

> I think that in no country in the civilized world is less attention paid to philosophy than in the United States. The Americans have no philosophical school of their own; and they care but little for all the schools into which Europe is divided, the very names of which are scarcely known to them.
>
> Yet it is easy to perceive that almost all of the inhabitants of the United States conduct their understanding in the same manner, and govern it by the same rules; that is to say, without ever having taken the trouble to define the rules, they have a philosophical method common to the whole people.
>
> To evade the bondage of system and habit, of family-maxims, class-opinions, and, in some degree, of national prejudices; to accept tradition only as a means of information, and existing facts only as a lesson to be used in doing otherwise and doing better; to seek the reason of things for one's self, and in one's self alone; to tend to results without being bound to means, and to aim at the substance through the form;—such are the principal characteristics of what I shall call the philosophical method of the Americans.

But if I go further, and seek amongst these characteristics the principal one which includes almost all the rest, I discover that, in most of the operations of mind, each American appeals only to the individual effort of his own understanding. [*Democracy in America*, II, bk. 1, i.]

For us, the consequences of the application of this method to nature and to society, above all as technology and bureaucracy, are so obtrusive that we sometimes find it hard to see anything else. But then, a century and a half ago, it must have taken much discernment to see that these nascent blessings and blights were indeed rooted in a national philosophical disposition—a disposition fusing specific American and universal democratic aspects, to form what Tocqueville understood to be a political community at once unique and exemplary.

Perhaps it might be argued that he makes a distinction without a difference, that wherever *homo sapiens* congregates, from lawless troglodyte to settled *polis*, from wandering tribe to territorial nation, there a way of thought has become incarnate in a community. The way and its communal appearance will differ: It may be the tacit, inbred maintenance of a grown tradition; it may be the devoted, continual exegesis of a God-given law; it may be the strenuous, correct adumbration of a certified ideology. Yet it is always a communal "philosophical method."

But there is indeed a deep distinction. These ways of using reason are not the *way of reason*. The mainstream of what I have circumscribed as the Western tradition is characterized by the deliberate, self-conscious activity of the original, personal faculty of thought, called *Reason* in the widest sense: "For although it is small in bulk, . . . if it is the chief and best part, it may even be what each one *is*." (*Nicomachean Ethics*, X, 1178 a.)

Now, what is so remarkable in Tocqueville's observation is that the people in whom this way has reached its worldly embodiment is also the people among whom "less attention is paid to philosophy" than among any other. This unreflective thought, this unreasoned use of reason, is what I here call *rationality*. It differs from the several other human modes of living sapiently by requiring an incessant application of the personal instrumental reason to the world, accompanied by an unremitting demand for articulate explanatory speech. And yet it is such reasoning and such speaking as can be embodied in a people and become a national habit. Insofar as the founders of the modern phase of the philosophical tradition intended just such an incarnation, America, the West's true West, is not, to be sure, the source, but certainly the first worldly home of philosophical modernity. However this modernity may be related to the tradition—whether as an enormous movement in its progress or as the large projection of a flaw lurking in its origins, or, again, as an abrupt corruption of the beginning[1]—it is on this continent that it found its exemplary realization.

Tocqueville's explanation for this phenomenon is that the ''philosophical method'' that he attributes to the Americans is peculiarly appropriate to their democratic condition, but that its invention is antecedent both to the theory and the actualization of democracy. It was first conceived in the sixteenth, published to the world in the early seventeenth, but domesticated here only in the later eighteenth century. The implication that lies at hand is that the method is somehow the source of democracy, but that is more than Tocqueville concludes, and truly too large an inference to make here.[2] He does state plainly, however, what it is that the two have in common. For as democracy is understood as the enfranchisement of the individual, so the chief characteristic of the method is ''that in most operations of the mind each American appeals only to the individual effort of his own understanding.''

Tocqueville was Frenchman enough to call this mode a method, and to call the method Cartesian. I would not call it a philosophical method so much as a philosophy *of* method, a mode of having methods. Nor is it, at least at its first appearance in America, Cartesian, or, for that matter, so very unconscious. The Founders, especially Jefferson, read a great deal, but they read Bacon and Locke and their French proponents rather than Descartes. The specifically Cartesian element—the programmatic mathematization of the world—was not yet explicit with them.[3] Yet, although in matters of human thought large outlines are almost always travesties, in this case, for once, a gross summary is peculiarly permissible, for the mode of rationality is precisely not a particular content but an assimilable habit. It is a true intellectual movement; or more to the point—it is *the* motion of the intellect peculiarly designed to become a movement.

The militant name this movement assigned to itself is *the Enlightenment.* I need hardly argue that we still live in that Enlightenment. To be sure, it has been subtilized by sophistications, tainted by reactions, and deepened by disillusionments, particularly with respect to its political effects. For, when this country was founded, the vein was:

> 1. Let the people by all means encourage *schools* and *colleges*, and all the means of *learning* and *knowledge*, if they would guard against slavery. For a *wise*, a *knowing* and a *learned* people, are the least likely of any in the world to be enslaved. [Rev. Samuel Webster's first commandment for a free people, 1777.][4]

A hundred years later:

> *Intellectual enlightenment* is a certain means to make men insecure, weaker-willed, more in need of companionship and aid, in short, to develop the *herd animal* in man.... The self-delusion of the mass on this point in every democracy is extremely valuable: the diminution and governableness of men is aspired to as "progress"! [Nietzsche, *Will to Power*, I, 129.]

And still another century later, the ultimate practical effects of the scientific Enlightenment are beginning to be in doubt, while as a mode of thinking about politics—as an urge toward the relentlessly radical application of rational schemes to the social condition[5]—it seems to feed on its failures.

It is its milder and more pervasive reign in education that I must attend to here, however, both in its bright and in its clouded consequences. The characteristics of students in the protracted Age of Enlightenment are known to every teacher: How multifariously "exposed" to and how little touched by experience; how quick and yet gullible in their sophistication; how full of the vocables of rationality and how thin of speech;

how stuffed with theory and how emptied of reflection! In short, how good and how endangered! What I wish to do in this chapter is to sketch certain fundamental facets of rationality and their inbuilt paradoxes that everywhere inform education and shape students. It would be foolish to attempt here the enormous philosophical labor of developing their hierarchy and relations; I shall, rather, attempt a descriptive complex. What makes the undertaking difficult is that to observe the facets of rationality is like trying to see one's own eye. Our habits of reason are so much of a piece with our functioning self that it is hard to discern their presuppositions. This mode of rationality is not *reason* itself, that is, a mental organ; nor is it *reasonableness*, that is, a moderating human disposition; nor is it *rationalization*, that is, a strenuous method for making things jibe with reason. It is much more elusive, in a way perfectly caught by William James in *The Sentiment of Rationality*:

> When enjoying plenary freedom either in the way of motion or of thought, we are in a sort of anaesthetic state in which we might say with Walt Whitman, if we care to say anything about ourselves at such times, "I am sufficient as I am." This feeling of the sufficiency of the present moment, of its absoluteness—this absence of all need to explain it, account for it, or justify it—is what I call the Sentiment of Rationality.

This most mobile mental mode is in the ordinary course a comfortable kind of oblivion, though it may eventually effect a diffuse sort of malaise. It is precisely because in it we are, as it were, in our element, that we find it so difficult to emerge from.

Facets of Rationality

"Self-thinking"—*Opinion.* I have borrowed an un-English but telling term from Kant: "*Self-thinking* means to seek the highest touchstone of truth in oneself (that is, in one's own reason); and the maxim always to think for oneself is Enlightenment." (*What is Meant by Getting One's Bearings in Thought*, Final Note.) To "think for oneself" is, especially in educational

contexts, the incessant demand, some educators forgetting themselves so far as to attempt to "make" people think for themselves. Is the phrase not redundant?[6] Is it not sufficient merely to think? Not so: As catching the first facet of rationality, the phrase does, indeed, have insistent significance. It signifies a conscious, self-assertive resistance to authority, a mental declaration of independence: "independence of mind," an assertion of individual sovereignty. *"Man's release from a tutelage, the blame for which is his own, is Enlightenment. His tutelage is his inability to make use of his understanding without guidance from another."* (Kant, *What is Enlightenment?*) The agent of this thinking is a *self*, an *ego*, namely, a *subject* that underlies all its own activity and continually says "I": "I think"; "I will"; "I feel." Its proper work, whether self-conscious or merely conscious, is to function—to be active in gathering and presenting, comparing and distinguishing, subjecting to rules and judging, some mental matter. It is before this supreme court of the self that all cases are ultimately brought for adjudication.

We speak of *the* self. Whose self? Is there reason to think that all selves are identical with *The Self*? There is not. It is in the very notion of a modern republic that each person, each ultimate judge, may well act as an individual, a being impenetrably opaque to all the others. Hence, a great multiplicity of opinion is expected—nay, welcomed: "It is a singular anxiety in some people that we should all think alike. Would the world be more beautiful were all our faces alike?" (Jefferson to Charles Thomson, 29 January 1817.) "As the Creator has made no two faces alike, so no two minds, and probably no two creeds," that is Jefferson's—and our—constant theme. We rejoice in multiplicity, or at the very least we feel obliged to tolerate, that is to say, bear it.

Yet it is equally in the notion of a republic that there must be a public realm in which the thought of all coincides to form a consensus. Jefferson is the true exemplar of the perennial enlightening optimist who is confident "that truth is great and will prevail if left to herself, that she is the proper and sufficient antagonist to error and has nothing to fear from conflict, unless by human interposition disarmed of her natural weapons, free argument and debate, errors ceasing to be dangerous when it is permitted freely to contradict them.'' (Virginia Act for Establishing Religious Freedom, 1786.) The cosmopolitanism of knowledge, the perfect diffusibility of ideas that are ''like fire, expansible over all space'' (to McPherson, 13 August 1813), is a canon of the Enlightenment, the necessary mediating link between the radical self-reference of individual reason and the universal progress of mankind.[7] The difficulty is, of course, that rationality is a mode, not a content, and although this mode is apparently irresistibly diffusible, no one truth need be confirmed by it, much less prevail.

Indeed, how could it? Each recalcitrantly independent thinker must regard his own views as universally true and all the others' thoughts as mere opinions. That is to say, where all think for themselves, each one's thought must be for every other mere opinion. But there follows this eventual public consequence: As everyone in an enlightened spirit of universal humanity sees himself reflected in other selves, he must come to view his own views as merely one of many, equally assailable, opinions. The logic of the mode of rationality precludes a truly public opinion; public motion must be either, as Locke proposes, in accordance with the forcelike vector of the larger mass of atomic judgments,[8] or by continual cession of individual thinking to form a necessarily compromised public consensus.

The consequences of this paradox of rationality to the world of learning are tremendous. On the one hand, there can be no authoritative teaching concerning the necessity, hierarchy, or even the content of studies. No faculty must ''impose its ideas'' on students or ''tell them what to think.'' Inasmuch as human beings have not yet learned to live without reference to truth, truth is retained, but as a private possession, a nonuniversal, uncontrollable, inarguable, unteachable truth, a truth ''true for me'' alone.

But something must be taught. Hence, a distinction arises and soon becomes ubiquitous. There are ''value judgments''—''subjective,'' rudderless, apologetic, but stubbornly unavoidable expressions of private opinion, those bastard presences of the classroom. On the other hand there are rigorous logical constructions and hard facts—objective, neutral knowledge, the less humane, the more respectable. But, of course, where a matter of any interest is concerned, that distinction is fully recognized as being absurdly inadequate. One solution is to turn all the matters of knowledge, subjective and objective, over to experts, whose thoughts and facts are to be trusted as if they were one's own. The existence of such banked knowledge makes it equally permissible for a student to admit, "I am totally ignorant" of some major human concern as to claim confidently the "we now know" the most difficult of matters. Indeed, "we" know the most remarkable things; for example, without the slightest benefit of quantum studies, "we," though we balk at a little calculus, seem to know that light travels both in waves and in particles—these objects are called wavicles. This peculiar kind of participatory knowledge is the substitute for a solidly formed common competence.

The pedagogical problem is how to protect the spontaneity of genuine thinking and prevent abdication to experts while developing the competence to gauge and use the experts' competence with some authority. Its resolution depends on recalling what is the real motive behind the insistence on thinking for oneself. It is the *will to certainty* that expressly possessed the founders of modernity, where the security of knowledge depended on its self-determination and its self-sufficiency. In the odyssey of such knowledge, the Siren song of certified science and the Scylla and Charybdis of radical self-reliance and radical skepticism—which is but certainty despaired of—are the unavoidable stations.

Now, in the premodern mode of thought the question of the validation of knowledge is circumvented. In the Platonic *Meno*, the obstructionist Meno indeed raises the question of the possibility, not of knowledge, but of inquiry, the human effort that is its precondition (80 d). But he is answered with a myth, the Myth of Recollection, which is not intended as a theory for certifying the possibility of inquiry, but as a device for making a learner effectively embark on it. Such learning, begun *in medias res*, from a basis of settled convictions and trusted observations, casts loose from the perplexities of "self-thinking" and alien influence. It goes for depth rather than certainty. It may proceed playfully—by likely stories, hypotheses, conjectures—producing slow conviction through common conversation. It forgoes narrow rigor (except as an occasional exercise) in favor of responsible vigor. As a complement, no college student should escape learning some carefully chosen fundamental skills that make it possible to judge, if not the experts' advanced development, then at least the presuppositions, of their knowledge. This way would be a return to thinking, not "for oneself," but thinking, merely.

Self-expression—Objectivity. Swift depicts his Laputans, those "large reckoners," the incarnations of the Cartesian philosophical method, as creatures with "one of their eyes turned inward, and the other directly up to the zenith." (*Gulliver's Travels*, III, ii.) They are blind to the middle distance.

It is the nature of the self to be self-involved, to regard, analyze, and eventually to express itself. Self-expression is the expansive complement of "self-thinking." On the one hand, the eye of the self is fixed on itself; on the other, it is trained on the skies. That is to say, the self is occupied not only with itself, but also with the knowledge and control of an outer object, nature. The subject has objects about which it has to be objective. Much of modern philosophy concerns the proper establishment of this subject–object relation.[9] The consequences to education are everywhere evident.

On the one hand, there is an explosive, if increasingly routine, fascination with that curious *imitatio dei* based on an expansive self-regard which is ubiquitously known as *creativity*. The artificial stimulation of spontaneity and originality is paradoxically thought to be necessary and to be capable of being institutionalized.[10] Schools are overwhelmed by the self-inconsistent demand to induce this mode of individual production. Responsible teachers are forced to double-deal programmatically. For example, they must use courses like the inescapable creative writing to inculcate the confining but indispensable practices of an art, which usually means beginning with the suppression of the more artless forms of self-expression. But then this whole Sisyphean substitute for serious apprenticeship is a hopeless enterprise that at once corrupts workmanlike discipline and depresses the sources of invention. No demand is more insistent, no result less satisfying. And yet it is an almost comically republican paradox that public attempts should be made to foster an intractably private individuality and its expression.

The correlate of subjectivity is objectivity—a strict demand to keep the person out of judgments, to attend to a given matter according to criteria so confining as to curtail the matter itself. In this aspect, students are taught vigorous methods for the collection and quantification of evidence as well as for the construction of arguments. From the indulgence of art to the strictness of science there seems to be no bridge for them, no middle ground on which to fix both eyes.

But the polar terms of explosive subjectivity and pinched objectivity *can* be removed from the pedagogical vocabulary. The first thing is by hook and crook to make students *speak*, and their object of study will soon unfold whatever intimacy, human significance, and even beauty it is capable of. If it is capable of none, it should be left until the immediate occasion for its use arises. Every teacher knows that there are nasty but necessary subjects that one forgets until one needs them, when they may even acquire a certain charm. On the other hand, studies should almost always be so chosen as to invite the students' shared participation. For example, the imaginative geometry so alluringly described by Sir Wilhelm Hamilton, in the quotation at the beginning of the chapter on Utility, produces a better common endeavor than a more efficient abstract algebra, simply because there is a handsome picture to show and discuss. Then, once students have been brought to *speak* (not to "express themselves" or "communicate"), it is of the essence that teachers should grant each student Heracleitus' request to listen "not to *me* but to my *speech*."

Teachers may notice out of the corner of the eye, so to speak, how and why a student talks, but the ear should be given strictly to the possible truth of the speech that is uttered. Students are much alive to this acknowledgment of their rational humanity, even when it takes the form of a thorough refutation. In that way, the breach instituted at the time of the Founding between the rational and the real studies, the studies of mere speech and of bald things, is reconciled. The clashing modes of subjectivity and objectivity are composed in the responsible attempt to speak the truth.

Theory—Theorizing. In observing the American preference for a certain kind of theory, Tocqueville distinguishes three grades, a pure, a middle, and an applied theory. The last, which consists of "methods of application and means of execution" is, he asserts, most at home in this country. ("Why the Americans are More Addicted to Practical than to Theoretical Science," *Democracy in America*, II, bk. 1, x.). I want to argue that it is the middle theory, intended to be composed of those "general truths that still belong to theory, but lead nevertheless by a straight and short road to practical results," that dominates and perplexes our lives. Not that anyone questions Tocqueville's observation, but there is no great educational paradox in the national devotion to applied science and technical training. The problem, if indeed there is one, would only be in the proper preparation for it.

Nor is that middle theory particularly problematic in mathematics and the sciences, where the distinction between the intermediate and the applied theory is fairly crisp. So, for example, physicists apply a calculus somewhat different from the pure theory based on a concept of continuity taught in mathematics; they use differentials, which allow them to calculate, as it were, with discrete least physical quantities. But what is more fundamental, the motives for the purer mathematical and scientific inquiry are fairly unclouded: Most scientists embrace the Baconian aphorism that "nature to be commanded must be obeyed" (*Novum Organum*, I, 3), which enjoins on their researches at least some phase of disinterestedness. It is when this middle kind of theorizing becomes the mode of thought applied to almost anything, particularly the human realm, both individual and social, that the problems arise.

Such theorizing consists of the production of mental artifacts, of rational constructions. It is, to be sure, an attempt to reproduce in the human realm the successes of the science of nature. But more fundamentally, it is an effort to apply universally the mode of rationality, usually in the shape of a *methodology*, that is to say, of a theory of method.[11] It is a frame of mind most certainly traceable to the generation of the Founders, who were confident that there were such human sciences, although they were then in their infancy. If one reads Condorcet (*Progress of the Human Mind*, Tenth Stage), on the application of the calculus of probabilities to the social sciences, on the necessity of perfecting their scientific terminology, and on the need for their further development, one might think that it was written not two hundred years but two days ago.

The peculiar difficulty of this kind of theorizing, which I touched on in the preceding chapter under "Educational Means," has to do precisely with its being a methodology. What students learn is the rationalization of an approach to a matter. The matter itself must be construed as a *problem* resoluble into components, for methods are in their nature and history analytical. For example, an innocuous-seeming introductory sentence to the study of the psychology of learning would be the finding, based on research, that "the processes of learning are extremely complex." Few students recognize how powerfully positive a statement this is. Yet compare the observation, based on self-inspection, that "the process of learning is deeply mysterious." It is no less true. It may stand at the beginning of an inquiry, but not of a theory. Theorizing requires approaching the matter in terms of complexity rather than of depth, as a clear-cut problem to which "problem-solving techniques" may be applied, so that, in Bacon's words, "the business be done as if by machinery." (*Novum Organum*, Preface.) Now, the difficulty is that this enterprise is intellectually ambiguous. It is the deepest intention of the Cartesian method (and that is what I have been describing) to turn all matter into a soluble problem and so to make *all* theory essentially useful; control is its ultimate motive. Hence, its students are forever suspended between contemplation and deliberation.

Teachers are only too familiar with the consequences. A theoretical technique is first attractive to students because it raises an expectation of potency. But then it never quite fits the present concrete case; it turns out to be, after all, mostly a sophisticated intellectual exercise, a kind of game, arid but fascinating. Students come away in an ensnared state of disenchantment, full of charmless knowledge and recalcitrant tools.

The classical meaning of the word *theory*, as I have pointed out before, is contemplation, "viewing." It is an activity whose end it is not to produce *a* theory, or to *solve* a problem, for to solve a problem is, after all, to dissolve the matter of the inquiry, since a solved problem is a matter of indifference. Theory is for the sake of seeing and presenting the object as it is in its very nature, for the "ardent love, the proud, disinterested love, of what is true."[12] This kind of theory corresponds to Tocqueville's highest grade. It depends, he says, on meditation. But, he observes, because of the incessant desire to utilize knowledge, "Nothing is less suited to mediation than the structure of democratic society."

I propose that it is a republican duty to prove Tocqueville, for once, wrong. It is precisely because we are masters of theorizing that we need theory. The founders of the democratic mode themselves meditated, albeit in that new spirit, at once aggressive and self-constrained, which harmonized with their intended practical conclusions. For instance, in beginning his reflection on the understanding, Locke characterizes it as capable not only of the skillful seizure of a prey, but also of a certain enjoyment of truth: "Its searches after truth are a sort of hawking and hunting, wherein the very pursuit makes a part of the pleasure." (*Essay Concerning Human Understanding*, Epistle to the Reader.) It therefore seems to me that teachers should make a careful distinction between the contemplative and the instrumental enterprise. They should set out for critical study a number of examples of the latter sort of theory, well chosen to give intellectual satisfaction, while initiating students into the unavoidable modern activity of theorizing. But there should also be times, frequent times, both for "hawking and hunting" and beyond that, for an even more meditative "mere" theory— for what Tocqueville called *mother knowledge*.

Mind—Experience. Who is there who does not believe himself to have a mind, "a mind of his own," who does not encourage others to use theirs, does not expect an education to train it? This mind (also called reason or understanding or head or brain) is the organ that performs the theorizing described above; it is the agent of rationality. Our ordinary way of referring to it is by way of material metaphor. We "keep" things in our minds, "sharpen" them, "grasp" things with them, and occasionally give people "a piece" of them. That metaphor goes back to those who established its character for us. Locke calls the mind an "empty cabinet" furnished by ideas let in by the senses (*Essay*, I, 2, 15), and also assigns to it those operations which we refer to as "handling ideas." It is entirely in order that Locke's direct successors, Jefferson among them, should go on to consider the mind simply as matter endowed with thought, a brain.[13]

Now, this mind, whose layout and operations have numerous descriptions, always reasons; that is to say, it makes rational linkages, such as deductive chains and generalized conceptions. But it must also have a secure, certain, immediate, and ultimate knowledge within itself—knowledge of "fact of existence" and of "axioms of logic." Such immediate knowledge is called *intuitive* (Locke, *Essay*, IV, ii, 1). Its warranty is *self-evidence*, inasmuch as it follows from nothing, being better known than anything else. In the beginning it is presented, with an unabashed sense of the parallelism, as the secular substitute for revelation: "Your own reason is the only oracle given you by heaven." (Jefferson to Carr, 10 August 1787.) It has a closely allied obverse and complement: a ready resignation as soon as rational revelation and experience both appear to fail, for instance in spiritual speculations. Thus Jefferson, when it comes to metaphysics, regularly reposes "his head on that pillow of ignorance which a benevolent Creator has made so soft for us." (To Reverend Story, 5 December 1801.)[14]

It has become our national habit to shuttle between positive knowledge and a determinedly comfortable curtailment of speculation. Particularly our political discourse is altogether shaped by the fact that the Founding principles come to us as truths held to be self-evident, as political axioms. Reference to such first principles is quite distinct from appeal to the implicit rules of custom, which "go without saying." Our principles are rational; they never go without saying and are constantly cited. But they can, and even must, go without reflection, for as axioms they are either immediately acceptable to all, or they grow threateningly precarious. The chief case, directly traceable to the Declaration of Independence, is, of course, our incessant reference to "our rights"; it is a reference that is thoroughly rational but not reflective. People rarely explain *why* they may have a right, but they argue powerfully *that* they have it.

Reason on its own, then, resorts to *self-evidence*, but, being essentially a tool, it needs a matter that supplies it with *evidence* on which to work. *Experience* is the term for the way of obtaining such evidence, which, significantly, applies to the evidence itself as well. Experience is commonly understood to arrive through organs of delivery, namely, the senses, and it comes through them packaged as "phenomena," "facts," "data," or "information." That is to say, experience is a way of receiving the world as *prepared* material for reasoning. It delivers wood, not trees. The "experiment," which puts nature on the rack to make her speak, is experience's most characteristic agency. Experience, especially sense experience, is therefore a term wholly within the mode of rationality.

Every teacher can testify how far this dual facet of rationality dominates education. On the one hand, some students under its influence will display a demonstrative inarticulateness, appropriate to those who know their moral, political, even mathematical, truths intuitively. Others are all too ready to repose on Jefferson's warm bed of ignorance and so to decline to inquire into questions of which they confidently know that they have no final answer.

At the same time, educational institutions bear the brunt of that perpetually starved need for "experiences," a need that is insatiable precisely because "experience" in its essentially contrived character can never fulfill the simple desire for sights or adventures of which it is the rationalized version.[15] Similarly, their response to the pressure to engage in "experiments" in order to make their offerings more exciting is doomed, for the educational experiment is an illogical conflation of the empirical method of trial and error with a desire for stimulation, which, unlike a scientific experiment, yields no convincing conclusions while wearing out institutional resources.

The resolution seems to me to be in refusing the terms. Schools are responsible for furthering the life of learning, not for delivering experiences. The former ought to be strenuous and invigorating enough to leave students at no loss for recreation, be it love and friendship, music and sports, alarums and excursions. The life of learning itself, on the other hand, demands the readiness to go beyond self-evidence and to become radically articulate. Wittgenstein ends his *Tractatus* with the famous demand, "Whereof one cannot speak, thereof one must be silent." Schools must make the complementary requirement, "Whereof one would express oneself, thereon one must *speak.*" And that means giving reasons.

Head—Heart. I am using this heading because its terms occur in what must be one of the most peculiar love letters ever written and sent, a letter that is also the epitome of this facet of rationality. It is Jefferson's famous epistle to Mrs. Cosway (1786). It was written right after he had seen her and her husband off from Paris: His head and heart have an argument, even an altercation. The head condemns his attachment to her as imprudent, the heart defends it as generous. The heart here lectures the head:

> When nature assigned us the same habitation, she gave us over it a divided empire. To you she allotted the field of science, to me that of morals. When the circle is to be squared, or the orbit of a comet to be traced: when the arch of greatest strength, or the solid of least resistance is to be investigated, take you the problem: it is yours: nature has given me no cognizance of it. In like manner in denying to you the feelings of sympathy, of benevolence, of gratitude, of justice, of love, of friendship, she has excluded you from their control. To these she has adapted the mechanism of the heart. Morals were too essential to the happiness of man to be risked on the uncertain combinations of the head. She laid

their foundation therefore in sentiment, not in science. That she gave to all, as necessary to all: this to a few only, as sufficing with a few.

Throughout the letter, the head stands for problem-solving, narrow calculation, abstemious self-sufficiency, careful correctness; the heart for human indulgence, generous impulse, large benevolence. The reason and the feelings are separate and distinct. The very act of locating them in different bodily organs separated in space drives that point home. That assignment of organs is, of course, not Jefferson's own. It is the stock of the Enlightenment into our own day.

Not only are head and heart distinct, they are opposed; the head is the would-be aristocratic oppressor of the heart's populace. And not only is it the oppressor, it is also—symbol of enlightened liberalism that it is—its own accuser and prosecutor. In this letter, as anywhere, it is the head that conducts the whole argument.

The head's understanding of the divisions of competences marks the most radical reversal of traditional roles. In the classical tradition, it is the intellect that is spontaneous (that is to say, immediate and original) and universal, in sum, public, while the passions are self-centered, passive, and essentially private.[16] In the letter it is just the reverse. Jefferson even goes so far as to credit the heart with the political Revolution and to turn the head into a pusillanimous Tory. Furthermore, the imagination, which is because of its formative powers traditionally close to the intellect, is now entirely at the service of the heart; a selfish will is instead the adjunct of the head. In brief, the head excludes, the heart encompasses.

The antagonism in time becomes both stale and violent. As the rule of reason grows pervasive, the "emotions"—significant replacement for the passions![17]—become exacerbated and attenuated at once and begin to posture:

Of the Suppression of the Passions.—If one continually denies oneself the expression of the passions ... that is, if one does not wish to suppress the passions themselves, but only their language and gesture: then one succeeds nonetheless in accomplishing precisely what one did not intend: the suppression of the passions themselves, at least their weakening and alteration. . . . Perhaps our present offers the strangest counterpart to that: I see everywhere, in life and in the theatre, and not least in all that is written, the sense of pleasure in all the *cruder* outbreaks and gestures of passion: a certain convention of passionateness is demanded—only not passion itself. [Nietzsche, *Gay Science*, I, 47.]

This "troublesome polarity" is all-intrusive and becomes acute in unbalanced times.[18] Education is expected to reform itself to alleviate it. The demand was already heard in the eighteenth century. Lord Kames, whose moral writings deeply influenced Jefferson in his youth, made then a still familiar complaint: "It appears unaccountable that our teachers generally have directed their instructions to the head, with very little attention to the heart."[19]

But is it so very unaccountable? This mode of rationality sees reason opposed to feeling, and it makes its assignments of competences accordingly, as Jefferson does: science to the head, morals to the heart; the rational, on the one hand, and on the other—the irrational. But irrationality is an embarrassment as a school subject, no matter what terms of rationality it may be presented under: self-expression, spontaneity, creativity, sensitivity, etc. How can the schools undertake the "culture of the heart" if morality has no connection with truth-seeking thought?[20]

At the bottom of the dilemma is the understanding of reason as a coldly wielded instrument, serving a selfish will. There *are*, however, alternative views: The intellect can be apprehended as a *passionate* capacity—the word *philosophy*, the love of wisdom, expresses that view. Again, the passions can be understood as having to thought a relation other than the politicized nexus of opposed interests. They can be considered precisely as *passive*, as affections that are invigorated by being mastered.[21] The paradox in the rational dichotomy is that human beings see themselves as oppressed by the very power of their mental tool. Well, then, the resolution never has and never will come from incessant attempts at equalizing and compensating and affirming the underprivileged faculty. What is wanted is a radical review of our capacity for thought, to see if it cannot resume its station at the center of human life.

Form over Substance

By *form* I here mean *mere* form, form as opposed to substance or content or the thing itself. It is what is empty and external about a matter, what defines and delimits a content. One useful phrase for the formal is that it is the *condition of the possibility* of an object, required so that it might exist, but not included in what it is. Chief among such formal conditions are the shaping and constituting operations of the mind.[22]

I shall argue that the effect of rationality on our lives is to formalize them in a gamut of aspects. Not only will my meaning become clearer as I sketch out some of them, but a swarm of additional examples cannot help but present itself to the reader.

First, it belongs to the very founding notion of rationality that to secure certainty the intellect severely delimits itself and forgoes certain inquiries. This self-imposed constraint runs directly contrary to the ancient protest that "we ought not to obey those who enjoin us as being human to think on human things, and as mortal on mortal matters." (Aristotle, *Nicomachean Ethics*, X, 1177 b.) Bacon's inquiry into the "true limits and bounds of reason," especially in divinity, Locke's setting of "horizons" for "all that boundless extent, that vast ocean of Being into which we let loose our thoughts," Kant's critical labor establishing the "limits of sense and reason"—these are all efforts in the same campaign of self-denial.[23] The effect is that attention is continually directed to the formal conditions of knowledge, that is to say, to the proper definition of the competence and extent of human thought. Jefferson, for example, the American incarnation of the Enlightenment, finally regards "some acquaintance with the operations of the mind" as the only useful part of metaphysics. (To Clark, 5 December 1825.)

These constraints are eventually accepted as expert mandates and reflected in all aspects of learning. Consequently, the approach to learning is formalized: Every intellectual enterprise must be certified before it is attempted; frames of reference must be given, terms defined; every book must be put in perspective by a preface; every pronouncement is to be prefaced by its apologia. The divisions of learning, too, are informed by limitations; specialization demands well-drawn boundaries and forgives only the most hesitant of transgressions. But above all, the matter itself is formalized; strenuous efforts are made to replace substance by logic and content by structure, even in the fine arts.

And, in general, there is the rage for abstraction, for sub-stituting what used to be called a *second intention*,[24] that is, the thought of a thought, for the thought of a thing:

> Democratic nations are passionately addicted to generic terms and abstract expressions, because these modes of speech en-large thought and assist the operations of the mind by en-abling it to include many objects in a small compass. A democratic writer will ... talk about *actualities* to designate in one word the things before his eyes at the moment. ... Democratic writers are perpetually coining abstract words of this kind, in which they sublimate into further abstraction the abstract terms of the language. [Tocqueville, *Democracy in America*, II, bk. 1, xvi.]

I nominate *methodology* as the most rampant example.

Second, method, process, manner, are preponderant over purposes and contents. Rationalization of means, standardiza-tion of form become centrally interesting. In making decisions, the mechanism matters more than the determination, even in private choices, say, in religious matters, where Jefferson's advice to his nephew has become the standard: "You are an-swerable not for the rightness but uprightness of the decision." (To Carr, 10 August 1787.) Not the content but the manner of the judgment matters: sincerity reigns. Similarly also in morals, the intention and the background of a deed, how it came about, is more regarded than the deed itself.

In education, methods, "curricular concepts," "delivery sys-tems," are the preoccupation. The subjects themselves are formalized, from notoriously frequently vacuous "Concepts and Methods of ..." courses to the pedagogically devastating replacement of geometry with its lovely imaginative content by abstract algebraic methods. Even achievement is formalized, for a quantitative statement of quality presents it in its most external aspect and, of course, eventually redefines it in those terms; when learning is measured, the measurable is eventually what is taught.

Third, there is that pervasive concern with utility as a preoccupation. It represents formalism in the present sense because it concentrates the attention on the means that make something possible, leaving aside the desired end as either predetermined or indeterminate. Appropriately, even the most solid and immediate object of pure utilitarianism, money, is also the most formal of possible goods; it is a *mere* condition of possibility. *Business* and its correlate *free time* are similarly formal; to be busy or to be "off" does not describe the substance of life.

Fourth, there is "The Future." The future is truly a mere form, a temporal form filled by no actual existence. The preoccupation with a worldly future is a deep feature of modernity; the notion that something is coming at us is ever present. Only, at the time of the Founding it was the earthly paradise of "indefinite progress," which Jefferson, with the aid of Condorcet, could envision with facility, while now we wonder

> what rough beast, its hour come round at last,
> Slouches towards Bethlehem to be born?
> [Yeats, "The Second Coming."]

But whether hopeful or harmful, something indefinite, for which we must prepare, is thought to be in the offing. This demand that we prepare students for "tomorrow's world" bedevils education, precisely because it enjoins attention to the most formal aspect of existence, its mere futurity. It produces a frame of mind quite distinct from prudence, which acts for clear ends with clever means. The results of this fixation on the future is that past and present substance is deprecated, and all efforts are centered on an indeterminable impending shape, like that old man of the sea, Proteus, who, when embraced, "will try to become everything." Yet, whenever that shape is thought to have been determined, say, by an expert, a "futurologist," it turns out to be as shifting as the present of which it is a selective projection.

Last and most pervasive in their formalistic consequences are the very political founding terms of this Republic. The principle of equality is a formal notion, whichever of the two chief contending interpretations is accepted. If equality is taken to mean equality of opportunity, it is obviously in itself merely a condition of possibility for becoming or gaining some possible good, perhaps to an unequal degree. If it is understood to require actual equality of result, it is similarly devoid of substance; the principle focuses public attention, not on a good, but on the comparison of its possession. Quantitative principles are always formal, that is, external to content, and sometimes even an inhibition on it; they do not so much encourage the production as they regulate the distribution of substance.

Liberty is our noblest and our most exemplary formal principle. It is nothing but the condition of possibility for being or doing or having something. It is noble precisely because it bestows nothing concrete at all. The claim that liberty is in itself a blessing is a mode of speech that shows our necessary concern with cherishing the *conditions* of our possible goods. But in fact the consequence of freedom in the public realm are to empty it of substance. This holds particularly in public education, for instance with respect to religion, where the Supreme Court has tended to hold that religious freedom as formulated in the First Amendment requires the schools to be cleared of positive religious practices.[25] But that exemplification of the formalism of liberty most germane to this inquiry is in the sphere of learning. Freedom of investigation, as advocated by Jefferson, ensures only the neutral possibility of a multiplicity of opinions; the emergence of any actual truth is left to precarious chance and its acceptance to private choice.

Finally, there is that most characteristic of American rights, the pursuit of happiness. This phrase speaks for itself; it almost seems designed to preclude *actual* happiness:[26] "It is strange to see with what feverish ardor the Americans pursue their own welfare, and to watch the vague dread that constantly torments them lest they should not have chosen the shortest path which may lead to it." (Tocqueville, *Democracy in America*, II, bk. 1, xviii.)

These and similar consequences of the mode of rationality, in turn exhausting and exhilarating, unsatisfying and stimulating in their relentless formalism, are the inherently appropriate and therefore irremediable features of a large instrumental public realm, such as this Republic was from the Founding intended to be. So much the more are they in want of a complement, a way that is free *without* rebuffing substance.

ATTEMPTED RESOLUTION OF THE PARADOX OF RATIONALITY

The Mode of Inquiry

Inquiry is a term of several meanings and much significance. It denotes questing, questioning, question-asking. It suggests intensity. It connotes a searching into things and a seeking out of truth. It intimates both the dis-ease of doubt and a trust in the possibility of satisfaction. I want to preempt it for the resolution of the dilemmas of Rationality.

I had used the term *inquiry* in the preceding chapter for the enterprise of reading the written tradition. I meant it to encompass all the ways of paying attention to texts, from mere etymology[27] to an account of the meaning of key words, from the plainest construction of a passage to its deepest interpretation, from a recognition of its references to a testing of its truth. To learn to do all this, that is, to learn to read texts of all sorts is, I have claimed, education in the prime sense. It is study. But reading can also lead beyond study.

In the monastic discipline of sacred reading, there appears a term that is very helpful here. It is *vacare lectioni*, "to be free for the reading," to be peculiarly open and receptive to its spirit.[28] In the secular discipline, too, the time should often come when the business of study gives way to the freedom of inquiry in the sense of this chapter: to the asking of questions.

What is a question?[29] To ask about asking is the most reflexive of all reflective questions and therefore the most crucial. But I shall shy away from its exposition here except in those merely descriptive terms, which bear directly on the dilemmas of rationality. It is, to begin with, much easier to say what a question, in my sense, is *not*. It is not a form of mere mental restlessness: The claim, so often made in prose and poetry that the quarry is nothing and the quest everything, turns the pursuit of truth into a mere exercise, which is, for all its strenuousness, rather idle. Why look when one does not mean to find? Again, question-asking need not always be that aggressively suspicious imputation of insufficient or bad motive called *questioning*, which we routinely encourage. (Although that sense does have an ancient precedent: in Greek, the philosophical term for the responsible cause or reason, and the legal term for blame or charge is the same: *aitia*.)

A genuine question is, when still within the questioner, an expectant vacancy, a receptive openness, a defined ignorance, and, above all, *a directed desire of the intellect*.[30] When launched, that is to say, uttered, it has a revealing double capacity: It can be asked either *of* a fellow human being or *about* things. When addressed to a human being, it is a demand for the communication, the sharing, of truth. When addressed to things, it serves notice that the world is held responsible, that it is thought to be able to answer, to speak out its depths, to be endowed with reasons. In either case, the condition of asking is the hope that the question can draw to us something we are in want of and that if ever we receive an answer we will be—for a while—fulfilled.

Question-asking therefore betokens a capacity deeper and more original than the instrumental reason. That latter faculty can be used or idled at will, can be handled like a tool to penetrate and strip and shape the world by discerning, dividing, distinguishing, analyzing, abstracting, comparing, contrasting, compounding. It can be trained to perform its operations habitually and to follow rational patterns called methods that enable it to perform its work in its own absence, so to speak. That deeper power is beyond manipulation, though not above encouragement. If it is recognized as that capacity for active receptivity or contemplation which is traditionally called the *intellect*,[31] then the *reason* represents its power-charged self-diminution. I am advocating a return to that intellect, or better, its reacknowledgment, for even in eclipse it is always, somehow, at work.

First, however, there is what might be called an "environmental" difficulty. The reason transforms the world; the intellect receives it. Thus, for contemplation to be possible it is necessary that there be something to view, something that is what it is originally, which has grown into being, which is *natural*.[32] It is the work of reason to rationalize the world. But such a remade world cannot be received and beheld; it must be seized and analyzed. The interest of the intellect requires the preservation of some nature, human and nonhuman, and particularly of something naturally beautiful, since the most ardent questions are incited by what is spontaneously attractive. Indeed, without an imagination informed by such beauty, the intellect remains inactive. Philosophy is indissolubly dependent on the conservation of a grown and given realm. If we were ever to succeed in transforming our whole world, including ourselves, into a "second nature," the intellect and its theory would indeed have to cease.

And second, there are institutional difficulties. Certainly there must be schools. There are binding practical reasons for institutionalizing study. Even meditation and contemplation, those most self-sufficient of all activities, are best done in a community: "The wise man is able to contemplate by himself ... though perhaps it is better if [even] he has co-workers." (Aristotle *Nicomachean Ethics*, X, 1177b.) But these necessities cannot mask the inherent awkwardness of institutionalized inquiry. For one thing, it is the most difficult of activities to direct, because it demands that the teacher provide discipline while forgoing dogma. It is also most apt to degenerate; precisely because it requires a certain deliberate elevation it can fall most precipitously into the abyss of pretentious talk and the absurdity of competitive question-raising. Scheduled reflection is almost a contradiction in terms.

Yet the enterprise also has its felicities. Suppose an institution is devoted to inquiry. When I say "devoted to" I do not mean that every moment is consecrated to the highest matters, for the bulk of time will certainly be absorbed by ordinary school studies and exercises, by recreations both innocent and not so innocent, and, unavoidably, by the intermittent inertia that always afflicts mortals at leisure to think. I mean that the school will be understood to exist for the sake of inquiry although it occur but occasionally, and that all the institutional ways will support that end. That purpose will, of course, constitute a real distinction from the *modern* academy. For example, the phrase *to make an original contribution* will lose its point, *research* will be replaced by search, *productivity* will go unrewarded—although there should be an obligation to the continual intramural, written articulation of thought, not as a contribution to the abstract world of learning, but as a benefit to the concrete present company.

Clearly, such a community can be expected to induce a certain decency, both intellectual and moral, and above all a readiness to listen to each other. I would even claim that precisely insofar as it encourages learning, a school fosters a most desirable civic virtue. It is formulable as something like a converse of Socrates' dictum that *excellence is knowledge: the desire to know is a virtue*, indeed a cardinal virtue in a modern republic. Therefore, a true school is in the happy position of being able to discharge a moral function through its own intellectual life.

Education in a Republic

A final question must nonetheless be posed: Is a reflective education, culminating in true inquiry, the kind of education I have made an effort to circumscribe, practically compatible with life in a modern republic?

First: it would not be sensible to deny that our lives are, and must be, largely devoted to practical and productive affairs. The notion of individual worldly effort is at the very root of our public realm. People must learn how to do things so they can live with "usefulness and reputation," and they must know enough about how things work to be competent judges of their "rights, interests, and duties." And, since our kind of business peculiarly defines a free time, people must learn how to make music (what is life without, say, a flute?), or pictures, or whatever gives pleasure. Therefore, reflective education can make a reasonable claim only to a part of a citizen's life, and most naturally to the college years. What occurs during this privileged interlude, this bracketed time, may—and indeed must—illuminate the rest of life. Collegiate learning is not impractical; it is *prepractical*. Impractical learning is the learning of abstractions, of thought separated and remote from its object, of generalizations too large, specifications too minute, and methods too rigid for the stuff they are intended to grasp. Prepractical learning is the immediate contemplation of the human and the natural world, aided by good books. To offer a bold if offensive example, political science is a frequently impractical discipline; political philosophy is an essential prepractical study.

Second: A school is not the world. And yet it is *a* world, a small republic of the intellect within the political community. Tocqueville observes that the survival of republican civilization depends on the vigor of such public associations of civil life: "Nothing, in my opinion, is more deserving of our attention than the intellectual and moral associations of America." (Tocqueville, *Democracy in America*, 2, bk. 2, v.) Such an association is, to be sure, a curtailed commonwealth; it is an unnatural city deprived of the dignity that attaches to communities into which people are born and from which they die their natural deaths. But it also has the advantages of these limitations. It is a place of leisure, that continuous opportunity for free activity that is so utterly different from "time off." Here, decisions are obviated; here, competition is suspended. Of course, agonies intrude, inequalities stand out in painful relief, and that blight on intellectual excellence, the desire to outdo each other, crops up. Naturally, shop, studio, stage, squash court, and swimming pool absorb much time—rightly, since ready recreation is one of the conditions of fresh thought. But in a true community of learning—not a training or service "facility"—all these diversions are incidental or ancillary to the common purpose, which is the life of learning. Places of this kind have always existed and exist now, and existence is proof enough of possibility. The point here is that life in such a school has, albeit in a blither fashion, the chief characteristic of the larger republic: that the more each person does in his own behalf, the richer is the public realm. But beyond demanding mutually profitable efforts, a community of learning concerns itself with a realm that is truly and *in its very nature* common and communicable; it is a place made to form the kind of friendship that comes from dwelling together in an *essentially* public realm. Therefore, a college worthy of the name will indeed provide the best possible preparation for life in a real republic, not so much as it is, but—a far more practical knowledge!—as it ought to be.

Third: Precisely because these little republics are not self-sufficient, they need a ground from which to draw life, and that ground is the larger republic. There is something inexpressibly foolish in the sight of an institution bent on ignoring or despising its own source. That educational communities should foster reverence for the Republic seems to me obvious. *In extremis*, radical reflection and civic reverence might indeed appear to be irreconcilable, yet the founder of all inquiry reconciled them precisely in his death: He was condemned to die because he refused to cease asking questions, and he was executed because he declined to flout his city's laws by running away. (Plato, *Apology* 37c; *Crito* 52c.) Under the political security the American Republic provides, however, no resolution so hard is called for: Indeed, a case can be made that a certain respectful admiration for our institutions is very likely to arise precisely in the course of a reflective education that takes place under their aegis.

Such an education is, to be sure, quite unable to devote itself to the fostering of mere traditions and mores. The academic study of rites and customs, absorbing though it may be, is, after all, only another scholarly discipline and *not* an initiation. If undertaken as such, especially in an interim community like a college, it soon degenerates into an exercise in nostalgia, a sentiment that unwittingly underscores the loss of a living tradition, for nostalgia literally means *return ache*, a desire to pass back into the past. But the past no more than the future is the object of the education here envisioned, although its chief means is indeed a tradition—the tradition of books discussed above. That study, however, is *not* nostalgic, because it does not aim at a return to the past but at its reappropriation for the present. The past matters, not as it has gone *before*, but as it has gone *into* the present. Such study of the past may even free the present for a new departure. And yet it might be said that the tradition of books is to the intellect what the traditions of customs are to the soul. The study of texts can induce a frame of mind analogous to the disposition of those who live in a tradition. For example, it can foster appreciation for the ingenious wisdom of founding efforts, patience with the slow development of depths and complexities, and a reluctance to wield the tool of reason too nonchalantly. Surely these intellectual habits are exactly such as are convertible into the civic virtues most needful at present. Yet far from being incompatible, they are precisely coincident with the desire to delve into all abysses and to leave no question unasked. A period given to inquiry is therefore indeed an appropriate preparation for republican responsibilities.

When I began by calling certain paradoxes of education in a republic *tragic*, I meant only that, like the heroic flaws of ancient tragedy, they are as exhilarating as they are appalling to the participant watchers, as appalling and as exhilarating as modernity itself. Each such paradox is an incitement to an inquiry and to a resolution intended not to collapse the paradox, but to recover its roots. All the resolutions together circumscribe an education that is uncompromisingly liberal, reasonably learned, and radically reflective. It seems to me also to be that education most apt to foster what is of the essence to this best of all practicable polities: that it be a republic of *incomparable equals*.

Notes

INTRODUCTION

1. Helen Wieruszowski, *The Medieval University* (Princeton: D. Van Nostrand Company, 1966), p. 191.

2. Historical works chiefly consulted: Lawrence A. Cremin, *American Education: The Colonial Experience , 1607-1783* (New York: Harper and Row, 1970); Bernard Bailyn, *Education in the Forming of American Society* (Chapel Hill: The University of North Carolina Press, 1960); Richard Hofstadter, *Academic Freedom in the Age of the College* (New York: Columbia University Press, 1955); Frederick Rudolph, *The American College and University: A History* (New York: Vintage Books, 1962).

3. Sir Richard Livingstone, the classicist, in Robert M. Hutchins, *The Conflict in Education in a Democratic Society* (New York: Harper and Brothers, 1953), p. 29.

4. *Desiderius Erasmus Concerning the Aim and Method of Education*, Classics in Education no. 19, William Harrison Woodward, ed. (New York: Bureau of Publications, Teachers College, Columbia University, 1964); *Vives: On Education, A Translation of the "De Tradendis Disciplinis,"* Foster Watson, trans. (Totowa, N.J.: Rowan and Littlefield, 1971, first published 1913). Two modern works of a humanist cast: Gordon Keith Chalmers, *The Republic and the Person; A Discussion of the Necessities in Modern Education* (Chicago: Henry Regnery Company, 1952); Mark Van Doren, *Liberal Education* (Boston: Beacon Press, 1959, first published 1943).

5. Not that the patron always paid much attention. Diderot slyly reminded his patroness, the Empress Catherine of Russia, that she had been known to pack such works away in a drawer; see the "Plan of a University" in *French Liberalism and Education in the Eighteenth Century: The Writings of La Chalotais, Turgot, Diderot, and Condorcet on National Education*, F. de la Fontainerie, trans. (New York: Burt Franklin, reprint, 1971).

6. The first expression of such an ambition I have come across, still uttered with a sense of its presumption, is by Torquato Tasso: "Only God and the poets deserve the name 'creator'." (Garin, II, 18; see complete reference in note 9.) In Jefferson's day, too, the word was still significant. The contemporary philosopher whom he admired most, Destutt de Tracy, writes, "Not

only do we never create anything, but it is even impossible for us to conceive what it is to create, if we understand by this word to make something of nothing." (*Treatise on Political Economy,* "Of Our Actions.")

7. Sometimes the source of this term in educational writings appears to be the equally devaluating *fact-value distinction* of the positivists.

8. Daniel Bell, *The Reforming of General Education* (Garden City, N.Y.: Anchor Books, 1968), p. 147.

9. I append some works that I do not mention at this point in the text. Together, these lists include a reasonable proportion of the classics in educational writing, but a diminutive part of all the existent works. In the case of classical works, the reference is to the standard paragraphing rather than to pages of editions that might not be at hand.

To begin with, two source books, the first a comprehensive book of snippets, the second an exceptionally fine bilingual (i.e., German and Latin) collection: Ellwood P. Cubberly, ed., *Readings in the History of Education* (Boston: Houghton Mifflin Company, 1920); Eugenio Garin, *Geschichte und Dokumente der abendlaendischen Paedagogik,* Ursula Schwerin, ed. (Hamburg: Rowohlt, 1966), vols. I-III (Cassiodorus to Locke); in addition, Roger Ascham, *The Scholemaster* (1570); Jean Le Rond d'Alembert, *Preliminary Discourse to the Encyclopaedia of Diderot* (1751); David Fordyce, *Dialogues Concerning Education* (1755); John of Salisbury, *The Metalogicon* (1159); John Stuart Mill, *Autobiography* (1873); Montaigne, *On the Education of Boys* (1580); Plato *Laws* VII (before 347 B.C.); Plutarch *On the Education of Children, Moralia, I* (ca. A.D. 100); Friedrich Wilhelm Joseph Schelling, *Lectures on the Method of University Studies* (1803); Herbert Spencer, *What Knowledge Is of Most Worth?* (1855); Thomas Aquinas, "The Divisions and Methods of the Speculative Sciences," *Commentary on Boethius'* "De Trinitate," *Questions V and VI* (ca. 1259); Giambattista Vico, *On the Study Methods of Our Time* (1709).

10. The American sources are: Richard Hofstadter and Wilson Smith, eds., *American Higher Education: A Documentary History* (Chicago: The University of Chicago Press, 1961), vol. I; S. Alexander Rippa, ed., *Educational Ideas in America, A Documentary History,* (New York: David McKay Company, 1969); Frederick Rudolph, ed., *Essays on Education in the Early Republic: Benjamin Rush, Noah Webster, Robert Coram, Simeon Doggett, Samuel Harrison Smith, Amable-Louis-Rose de Lafitte du Courteil, Samuel Knox,* (Cambridge: Harvard University Press, 1965); Wilson Smith, ed., *Theories of Education in Early America 1655-1819* (Indianapolis: The Bobbs-Merrill Company, 1973).

See also: Allen O. Hansen, *Liberalism and American Education in the Eighteenth Century* (New York: Octagon Books, 1965), a review of early American works on education; Abraham Blinderman, *American Writers on Education Before 1865* (Boston: Twayne Publishers, 1975), containing many quotations.

11. I have counted seven such umbrella terms on two pages of a fairly recent

book on education (Bell, *Reforming of General Education,* pp. 162-63).

12. As related in William Bradford, *New England's Memorial.*

13. Jefferson's writings on education consist almost entirely of legal texts, reports, and letters. The chief items are: "Bill 79 of 1799 for the 'More General Diffusion of Knowledge,'" proposing a public school system consisting of "hundred" (ward) schools, "grammar" (secondary) schools, and a college (William and Mary), together with its thorough exposition in the *Notes On the State of Virginia* (Queries XIV and XV); Letter to Peter Carr, 10 August 1787, on college studies; Letter to Peter Carr, 7 September 1814, outline of a complete institutional plan from elementary to professional schools; also the corresponding "Bill of 1817"; "Report of the Commissioners Appointed to Fix the Site of the University of Virginia," 1 August 1818 ("Rockfish Gap Report"), Jefferson's most extensive statement on the aims and contents of both "primary" and "higher" education. Letter to Joseph C. Cabell, 3 February 1825 (with Madison's moderating reply of 8 February 1829), on the prescription of texts for the study of government; also the "Minutes of the Board of Visitors of the University of Virginia," 4 March 1825; these texts are to be found in Cabell, published letters, Conant, *Crusade,* and Honeywell, as cited in this note; the last three are collected in Arthur Bestor, "The Reading of Thomas Jefferson," in *Three Presidents and Their Books* (Urbana: University of Illinois Press, 1955), pp. 39-44.

Collections and scholarly works: Herbert B. Adams, *Thomas Jefferson and the University of Virginia* (Washington, D.C.: Government Printing Office, 1888); James B. Conant, *Thomas Jefferson and the Development of American Public Education* (Berkeley: University of California Press, 1962); *Early History of the University of Virginia as Contained in the Letters of Thomas Jefferson and Joseph C. Cabell* (Richmond: J. W. Randolph, 1856); Roy J. Honeywell, *The Educational Work of Thomas Jefferson* (Cambridge: Harvard University Press, 1931); *Thomas Jefferson and Education in a Republic,* Charles F. Arrowood, ed. (New York: McGraw-Hill Education Classics, 1930; Michigan: Scholarly Press, 1970).

14. Merrill D. Peterson, *The Jefferson Image in the American Mind* (New York: Oxford University Press, 1960; reprinted 1970), pp. 238-44.

15. *A Turning Point in Higher Education; the Inaugural Address of Charles William Eliot* (Cambridge: Harvard University Press, 1969), p. 2.

16. H. I. Marrou, *History of Education in Antiquity* (New York: Mentor Books, 1964, first published in 1948), pt. 2, ch. VIII, and p. 528, n. 3.

17. For a discussion of *encyclopaedia,* and of the liberal arts, see chapter 2. For the *egkyklios paideia* as education for boys, see Quintilian I, x; for the liberal arts taught to young men, Hugo St. Victor, *Didascalicon* (Garin, I, pp. 164 ff.). For the philosophical purpose of the arts, see Plato, *Republic* VII; Isocrates, *Antidosis* 270 ff. (the more significant because so perfunctory), and again Hugo (Garin I, pp. 188 ff.)—a tiny sample. Incidentally, Hugo's jewel of a treatise on learning (first half of the twelfth century) bears the full title *Didascalicon de studio legendi* or *Teaching Manual on the Pursuit of Reading.*

18. An invaluable series of sources, especially in American education, is the Classics in Education. It is published by the Bureau of Publications, Teachers College, Columbia University, New York. See especially: Francis Wayland, "Thoughts on the Present Collegiate System" (1842), *The Colleges and the Public, 1787-1862* no. 15, Theodore Rawson Crane, ed. (1963), *ibid.* for the "Yale Report" (pp. 83 ff.) and Wayland's other writings (pp. 112 ff.). See also: *The Age of the Academies* no. 22, Theodore R. Sizer, ed. (1964); *Benjamin Franklin on Education* no. 14, John Hardin Best, ed. (1962); *The Republic and the School; Horace Mann on the Education of Free Men* no. 1, Lawrence A. Cremin, ed. (1957).

On the enormous number of post-Revolution college foundations, see Hofstadter, *Academic Freedom*, p. 211. Several of these were prevented by their charters from "requiring or enforcing any religious test," and one, at least, even had a principal who was not a clergyman, John McDowell of St. John's College, Annapolis, Maryland, chartered 1784; the charter, especially in its draft version, has wording similar to that of Rhode Island College (1764), a great colonial example of religious toleration. (Hofstadter and Smith, *Documentary History,* pp. 134-36.) The latter school (later Brown University) was founded by Baptists, to whom the separation of Church and State was particularly dear.

19. For the difference between liberal and general education, see Bell, *Reforming of General Education*, p. 8, where the distinction is ignored; Van Doren, *Liberal Education*, "Preface to Beacon Press Edition," where the distinction is made; Russell Thomas, *The Search for a Common Learning: General Education, 1800-1960* (New York: McGraw-Hill Book Company, 1962), pp. 104, where the distinction is deprecated.

See also: Sidney Hook, Paul Kurtz, Mario Todorovich, eds., *The Philosophy of the Curriculum; The Need for General Education* (Buffalo: Prometheus Press, 1975).

Only one school, St. John's College at Annapolis and Santa Fe, has reinstituted a full-scale, stable liberal arts program combined with readings in the Western textual tradition, the "New Program" of 1937.

20. Cabell, *Letters,* pp. 304 ff.

21. Albert J. Nock, *The Theory of Education in the United States* (Chicago: Henry Regnery Company, 1932).

CHAPTER 1

1. *John Locke's "Of the Conduct of the Understanding,"* Classics in Education no. 31, Francis W. Garforth, ed. (1966), p. 53. The notion of a general training of the faculties, which I shall have occasion to criticize in Chapter 2, is recognized under the term, *formal discipline;* see Walter B. Kolesnick, "John Locke and the Theory of Formal Discipline," *Catholic Educational Review* 57, no. 3 (March 1959): 185, 187.

For the Euclid anecdote, see Thomas L. Heath, ed., *The Thirteen Books of Euclid's Elements* (New York: Dover Publications, 1956), I, p. 3. Euclid was said to have been "by preference a Platonic and attached to that philosophy," p. 2, n. 1.

2. Hermann Diels, *Fragmente der Vorsokratiker* (Berlin: Weidmannsche Verlagsbuchhandlung, 1954), II, p. 306, 27.

Rousseau frankly encourages his Émile to learn sciences, for example, astronomy, in a utilitarian frame of mind, and to ask always "What is it good for?", exactly the question Euclid is said in the anecdote to scorn. Such a disposition gives the educator hidden control: "As soon as we have managed to give our pupil some idea what the word 'utility' means, we have another strong hold on him." (bk. 3.)

3. For example, Isocrates, *Antidosis*, 181: "Certain of our ancestors long before us saw that arts had been established concerned with many other things, but nothing had been prescribed for the body and the soul. So they devised a pair of disciplines and left them to us: training for the body, part of which is gymnastics, and for the soul, philosophy, . . . not much distinguishing the two kinds of education from one another but using similar sorts of teaching, of exercise and of other disciplines."

4. Again the source is Stoic; see Cicero, *On Duties*, II, iii, "*Utile*," based on the Stoic Panaetius.

5. I believe that the use of educational institutions to train students to solve social problems was first envisioned as a national aim (as distinct from an educationists' plea) in the influential *Report of the President's Commission on Higher Education* of 1947 (*Higher Education for Democracy*, Washington, D.C.: U.S. Government Printing Office, 1947), vol. I, ch. I, "Toward the Solution of Social Problems," p. 20. For the much older social use of the lower schools, see John D. Pulliam, *History of Education in America* (Columbus: Charles E. Merrill Publishing Company, 1976), pp. 157-59.

6. For instance, by Newman, *The Idea of a University*, Discourse VIII, 10, for whom a gentleman is simply "one who never inflicts pain." Also Leo Strauss, "Liberal Education and Mass Democracy," in *Higher Education and Modern Democracy*, Robert A. Goldwin, ed. (Chicago: Rand McNally and Company, 1967), pp. 73-96, in which a gentleman is understood to be a sufficiently leisured free man who has governing responsibilities.

7. For example, by Francis Wayland and Jonathan Baldwin Turner in *The Colleges and the Public*, pp. 143, 185. Herbert Spencer, whose *Education: Intellectual, Moral, and Physical* (1860) was much read in America, completed the utilitarianization of education by interpreting the ornamental as a specious form of the socially useful; *Herbert Spencer on Education*, Classics in Education no. 30, Andreas M. Kazamias, ed., p. 122.

8. Frederick Rudolph, ed., *Essays on Education in the Early Republic: Benjamin Rush, Noah Webster, Robert Coram, Simeon Doggett, Samuel Harrison Smith, Amable-Louis-Rose de Lafitte du Courteil, Samuel Knox* (Cambridge: Harvard University Press, 1965), p. 56.

9. Rush, "Thoughts upon Female Education, Accommodated to the Pres-

ent State of Society, Manners, and Government in the United States of America," Rudolph, ed., *Essays on Education*, p. 33; Webster, p. 71.

10. Jefferson put in no less than three hours a day of practice on the "fiddle" on the very eve of the Revolution; see Helen Cripe, *Jefferson and Music* (Charlottesville: University Press of Virginia, 1974), p. 6. The depreciation of music in education is directly connected with the denial of a theory both of the soul and of music, such that music can affect the moral disposition; see for example, Eduard Hanslick, *Vom Musikalisch-Schoenen, Ein Beitrag zur Revision der Aesthetik der Tonkunst* (Wiesbaden: Breitkopf und Haertel, 1966; first published in 1854), pp. 125 ff.

11. *Some Thoughts Concerning Education* forms the chief part of *The Educational Writings of John Locke*, James L. Axtell, ed. (Cambridge: The University Press, 1968), pp. 109–325.

12. In George Elder Davie, *The Democratic Intellect: Scotland and Her Universities in the Nineteenth Century* (Edinburgh: University Press, 1964), p. 155.

13. *American Education and Vocationalism: A Documentary History 1870–1970*, Classics in Education no. 48, Marvin Lazerson and W. Norton Grubb, eds. (1974), p. 127.

14. Wilhelm Goerdt, ed., *Die Sowjetphilosophie, Wendigkeit und Betimmtheit, Dokumente* (Darmstadt: Wissenschaftliche Buchgesellschaft, 1967), p. 301.

15. Karl Marx, *The Economic and Philosophic Manuscripts of 1844*, Dirk J. Struik, ed. (New York: International Publishers, 1964), p. 111.

16. *American Education and Vocationalism*, p. 164.

17. Ibid., p. 164 (Council), pp. 124–26 (Commission).

18. A savage attack on vocationalism is to be found in Veblen's *Higher Learning in America*, ch. 7. He points out that the ever-fateful elective system is largely responsible for the invasion of institutions of higher learning by utilitarianism: Vocational electives drive out traditional scholarly subjects. He is protective of the kind of scholarly knowledge for knowledge's sake that I have listed under "Educational Inutility." It seems to me distinct from the liberal education I shall defend later.

19. William James, "The Social Value of the College Bred," *In Pursuit of Awareness; The College Student in the Modern World* (New York: Appleton-Century-Crofts, 1967), p. 41; Angela Thirkell, *The Duke's Daughter*, ch. 10.

20. *Die Sowjetphilosophie*, p. 299.

21. Rudolph, ed., *Essays on Education*, pp. 9, 17, 20. *The Republic and the School: Horace Mann on the Education of Free Men*, Classics in Education no. 1, Lawrence Cremin, ed., "Political Education," pp. 89–97; on vocal music, p. 11. Priestley had proposed a course of political studies for English "gentlemen designed to fill the principal stations of active life" in 1765, in *An Essay on a Liberal Education for Civil and Active Life*; see Priestley's *Writings on Philosophy, Science and Politics*, John A. Passmore, ed. (New York: Collier Books, 1965), pp. 285 ff.

22. Harvey Flaumenhaft, "Hamilton on the Foundation of Government,"

The Political Science Reviewer VI (Fall 1976), p. 152. Adam Smith's chapter heading "Of the Beauty which the Appearance of Utility bestows upon all the Productions of Art . . . " (*The Theory of Moral Sentiments*, IV, 1) is cited there.

23. On the difficult relation of the revolutionary Founders to the stable institutions they advocated, see David Tyack, "Forming the National Character; Paradox in the Educational Thought of the Revolutionary Generation," *Harvard Educational Review* 36, no. 1 (Winter 1966): 37, an article of great help to this and the following headings. Also, Hannah Arendt, *On Revolution* (New York: The Viking Press, 1965), "The Revolutionary Tradition," pp. 217 ff.

24. The textbook episode will necessarily be mentioned a number of times. For the documents, see Arthur Bestor, *Three Presidents and Their Books* (Urbana: The University of Illinois Press, 1955), pp. 39-44.

25. Quoted in full in George F. Kennan, *Democracy and the Student Left* (Boston: Little, Brown and Company, 1968), pp. 3-4.

26. Noah Webster, in Rudolph, ed., *Essays on Education*, p. 56. The double argument for deprecating most book learning, that it hinders both independent thinking and mechanical aptitude, belongs to a romantic context; for example, Rousseau allows his Émile, a boy able "to draw all his knowledge from himself," only one book in his library—not Aristotle, not Pliny or Buffon, but *Robinson Crusoe*, which plays the role of a do-it-yourself manual for the noble young savage.

27. Arendt, *Revolution*, p. 221. A small exemplification occurs in the quotation below from the "Rockfish Gap Report." An omitted clause concerning the *indefinite*, as opposed to the *infinite* progress of mankind apparently derived directly from Condorcet's *Sketch for a Historical Picture of the Progress of the Human Mind*, Tenth Stage.

28. Of course, college students participated enthusiastically in revolutionary activity, but in the national cause, on the side of the patriots, the future establishment; see Richard Hofstadter, *Academic Freedom, in the Age of the College* (New York: Columbia University Press, 1955), p. 206.

29. Joel Barlow, *Prospectus for a National Institution to be Established in the United States* (Washington, D.C.: S. H. Smith, 1806), p. 5.

30. See Rudolph, ed., *Essays on Education*, passim.

31. The formula describing the sectarian cast of the colonial Protestant colleges was "toleration with preferment"; see Jurgen Herbst, "The Eighteenth-Century Origins of the Split Between Private and Public Higher Education in the United States," *History of Education Quarterly* 15, no. 3 (Fall 1975): 274. For financing, see Frederick Rudolph, *The American College and University; A History* (New York: Vintage Books, 1962), p. 189. For the antagonism of private and public schools on a primary and secondary level, see Frank Tracy Carlton, *Economic Influences upon Educational Progress in the United States 1820-1850* Classics in Education no. 27 (first published in 1908), p. 81.

32. Pierre Samuel du Pont de Nemours, *National Education in the United*

States of America, B. G. du Pont, trans. (Newark: University of Delaware Press, 1923), p. xiii. Washington even offered shares privately toward such an enterprise. (To Robert Brooke, 16 March 1795; 1 September 1796.) Among the enlightened educators it was only Priestley who pointed out the dangers of state education: "An Essay on the First Principles of Government," in *Writings*, pp. 305 ff. But then he was still living in England.

33. The crucial event in making equal educational opportunity the primary issue before the public is, of course, the Supreme Court decision in *Brown* v. *Board of Education* of 1954, which overturned the "separate but equal" doctrine as a justification for racially segregated schools. It placed unprecedented reliance on the findings of social scientists for determining the actual equality of an educational setting: *The Supreme Court and Education*, Classics in Education no. 4, David Fellman, ed. (1976), p. 138. It is often pointed out that this decision, whatever its practical consequences may be, is one of the foremost instances of the educative functions of the law: involuntary segregation no longer has respectable public defenders. This is an aspect of the law Jefferson showed little explicit interest in, although his great bills all had educative preambles,—ironically, in view of his anti-Platonism— exactly like those advocated in Plato's *Laws* (IV, 721 d ff.).

T. S. Eliot, in his essay "The Aims of Education" (1950), gives a critique of the notion of equal opportunity, arguing that it inevitably leads to more state control and that, in turn, to vocationalism; *To Criticize the Critic* (New York: Farrar, Straus and Giroux, 1965), pp. 101 ff.

34. Nannerl O. Keohane, "Virtuous Republics and Glorious Monarchies: Two Models in Montesquieu's Political Thought," *Political Studies* 20 (December 1972): 388, 395. Nonetheless, the early writers cite the passage: Rudolph, ed., *Essays on Education*, pp. 66-125.

Jefferson's criticisms of Montesquieu were reinforced by Destutt de Tracy's *Commentaries on Montesquieu*, which Jefferson partly translated; Adrienne Koch, *The Philosophy of Thomas Jefferson* (New York: Columbia University Press, 1943), pp. 59, 152.

35. The chief source of the principle of universal benevolence and the moral sense on which it is based is, at least for Jefferson, the work of Lord Kames, which he particularly admired. See especially Kames's *Essays on the The Principles of Morality and Natural Religion*, paras. 913 ff., 935 ff., in *British Moralists*, L. A. Shelby-Bigge, ed. (New York: Dover Publications, 1965), II, 302 ff.

However mild early republican virtue may have been, it had a good deal more expansiveness in it than Franklin's sober program for moral self-perfection, which he set out in his *Autobiography* (Continuation, 1730). His thirteen virtues, beginning with Temperance ("Eat not to dullness; drink not to elevation") to Humility ("Imitate Jesus and Socrates") are an almost programmatic repudiation of the nobility of virtue in favor of taut control. But then, Franklin's robust *joie de vivre* could support such a morality.

36. Rudolph, ed., *Essays on Education*, pp. xix, 11.

37. Merrill D. Peterson, *The Jefferson Image in the American Mind* (New York: Oxford University Press, 1960; reprinted 1970), pp. 243-44.

38. Stephen Simpson, *A Manual for Workingmen*, referred to in *Economic Influences*, Classics in Education no. 27, p. 54.

39. *The Colleges and the Public, 1787-1862*, Classics in Education no. 15, Theodore Rawson Crane, ed. (1963), p. 57.

40. Koch, *Philosophy of Thomas Jefferson*, pp. 54 ff.

41. *Report of the President's Commission on Higher Education*, p. 61.

42. "Rockfish Gap Report." To my knowledge, the first description of a polity where work is constitutionally liberal is Thomas More's *Utopia*. Locke again leads in making a craft an integral part of the education of gentlemen intended for affairs of state, and he very cleverly attributes this custom to the ancients, though perforce omitting the Greeks in his examples (*Thoughts*, 205-6). The philosophical elevation of laborious service as inhibited desire that, being denied the quiescence of consumption, continually and triumphantly forms the world in its own image, is to be found in Hegel's *Phenomenology*, 4 A, "Lordship and Bondage." Josef Pieper, in a book with much bearing on this chapter and my last, separates work from liberal leisure somewhat more harshly than I should. (*Leisure: The Basis of Culture* [New York: Mentor Books, 1964], pp. 24 ff.)

CHAPTER 2

1. For a small example: In Plato's *Timaeus* are presented, playfully, the foundations of model-making (not, significantly, by Socrates); Nicole Oresme, in his fourteenth-century *Treatise on the Uniformity and Difformity of Intensions* displays the origin of physical graphs. Descartes's *Rules for the Direction of the Mind* deals with the question of the mathematical representation of physical characteristics; the article "Diagrams" in *The Scientific Papers of James Clark Maxwell* (New York: Dover Press, 1965), pp. 647 ff., considers and classifies various diagrams of physics.

2. Eugenio Garin, *Geschichte und Dokumente der abendlaendischen Paedagogik*, Ursula Schwerin, ed. (Hamburg: Rowohlt, 1966), 2:193.

3. As in that little anthropological masterpiece by Elenore Smith Bowen, *Return to Laughter*, ch. 2.

4. The title of Abelard's book of unresolved arguments, pro and con, about theological topics, first half, twelfth century.

5. Moses I. Finley, *The World of Odysseus* (New York: The Viking Press, 1965, rev.), p. 29.

6. Ernst Robert Curtius, *Europaeische Literatur und Lateinisches Mittelalter* (Bern: Francke Verlag, 1948), p. 397. This work is a magnificent treatment of the Western literary tradition and its terms.

7. Claude Lévi-Strauss, *Tristes Tropiques* (New York: Atheneum, 1975), pp. 37 ff.

8. Garin, I, 102.

9. Curtius, p. 260, n. 2.

10. Curtius, p. 63.

11. See also Garin, III, 8 ff.

12. *French Liberalism and Education in the Eighteenth Century: The Writings of La Chalotais, Turgot, Diderot, and Condorcet on National Education*, F. de la Fontainerie, trans. (New York: Burt Franklin, reprint, 1971).

13. Franklin, "Proposals Relating to the Education of Youth in Pennsylvania," n. 13, in *Benjamin Franklin on Education*, Classics in Education no. 14, p. 140; J. S. Mill, *Autobiography*, early years; a humanist on the impracticality of beginning with Greek: Battista Guarino, "On the Order of Teaching and Study 3," in *Vittorino de Feltre and Other Humanist Educators*, Classics in Education no. 18, William Harrison Woodward, ed. (1963), p. 167; on English language study: *Richard Mulcaster's Positions*, para. 51, Classics in Education no. 44, Richard DeMolen, ed. (1971), p. 61; also *The Educational Writings of John Locke*, James L. Axtell, ed. (Cambridge: The University Press, 1968), p. 189.

14. On Capella, see William Harris Stahl, *Martianus Capella and the Seven Liberal Arts* (New York: Columbia University Press, 1971), I; on the *trivium*, see Curtius, p. 47; one additional book should be mentioned: Isidore of Seville, *Etymologies or Origins* (7th century).

15. Saint Thomas Aquinas, *The Division and Methods of the Sciences, Questions V and VI of His Commentary on the* De Trinitate *of Boethius*, Armand Maurer, ed. (Toronto: The Pontifical Institute of Medieval Studies, 1963), p. 11, Qu. V, Art. 1, Reply to 3. Also, Hugo St. Victor, Garin I, 188.

16. Garin I, 21, 155.

17. For example, Tom Paine's *Age of Reason*; *enlighten* was one of Jefferson's favorite verbs.

18. Curtius, p. 259.

19. For example, Comenius, *The Great Didactic*, Classics in Education no. 33, 6 and 45, pp. 68, 87. The Master Hartlip to whom Milton's essay is addressed was a propagator of Comenius' pedagogical doctrines.

20. Allen G. Debus, *Science and Education in the Seventeenth Century; The Webster-Ward Debate* (New York: American Elsevier Publishing Company, 1970), p. 103.

21. The foretaste of these romantic attacks on study itself came in the contempt for scholastic learning expressed, for instance, by Descartes (*Discourses on Method*, I).

22. Richard Hofstadter, *Anti-Intellectualism in American Life* (New York: Alfred A. Knopf, 1964), p. 165.

23. Dumas Malone, *Jefferson and the Rights of Man; Jefferson and His Time* (Boston: Little, Brown and Company, 1951), II, 211, 287.

24. *Spirit*: In its inception, this view did indeed occasion a most serious examination of texts for that recovery of the appearances of the Spirit that must precede the writing of a rational or "conceived" history (Hegel, *Phenomenology of the Spirit*, ch. 8). But that deep, difficult, and system-bound effort is soon corrupted into a shallower historicism.

The phrases are quoted from Alfred North Whitehead, *The Aims of Education*, ch. 6. The Arnold Toynbee phrases in the text come from "Higher Education in a Time of Accelerating Change," *Campus 1980*, Alvin C. Eurich, ed. (New York: Delta Books, 1968), pp. xix–xxiv.

25. By far the largest number of quotations in the following sections is from letters. The major edition will be *The Papers of Thomas Jefferson*, I– , Julian P. Boyd, ed. (Princeton: Princeton University Press, 1950–). The completed editions are listed in Malone, *Jefferson the Virginian; Jefferson and His Time*, I, 459-61. Excellent selections: Adrienne Koch, ed., *The American Enlightenment*, The American Epochs Series (New York: George Braziller, 1965), pt. 3; Bernard Mayo, ed., *Jefferson Himself* (Charlottesville: University of Virginia Press, 1970); Saul K. Padover, ed., *A Jefferson Profile* (New York: The John Day Company, 1956).

26. The role of the classics in early America and in Jefferson's life: Richard M. Gummere, *The American Colonial Mind and the Classical Tradition* (Cambridge: Harvard University Press, 1963); Karl Lehman, *Thomas Jefferson, American Humanist* (Chicago: The University of Chicago Press, Midway Reprint, 1973). The Fordyce quotation comes from David Fordyce, *Dialogues Concerning Education* (Cork: Phineas and G. Bagnell, 1755). Franklin cites the work in his "Proposals" as generally attributed to Hutcheson.

27. Evidence for Jefferson's classical reading: Gilbert Chinard, ed., *The Literary Bible of Thomas Jefferson; His Commonplace Book of Philosophers and Poets* (Baltimore: The Johns Hopkins Press, 1928; reprint, New York: Greenwood Press, 1969), especially pp. 2, 14, 27, 207; on pronunciation: Lehman, *Jefferson, Humanist*, p. 98; explication of *logos: reason* or *mind* (not *deed*, as in Goethe's *Faust* 1237), to Adams, 11 April 1823; exposition of Theognis' poem: to Adams, 28 October 1813.

28. H. Trevor Colbourn, "Thomas Jefferson's Use of the Past," *The William and Mary Quarterly* 15 (1958): 56-70.

29. See Norbert Sand, "The Classics in Jefferson's Theory of Education," *Classical Journal* 40, no. 2 (November 1944): 92-98.

30. Here I am happily seconded by the greatest classical scholar of this century, A. E. Housman, who incidentally gives a very dry and measured— and consequently convincing—argument: The classical languages quicken appreciation and refine discrimination for those naturally qualified to profit from them, nothing more; *Selected Prose* (Cambridge: University Press, 1961), "Introductory Lecture," pp. 9 ff.

31. Jefferson on colonial buildings: *Notes on Virginia*, Qu. XV. For classicism in America, see Howard Mumford Jones, *O Strange New World* (New York: The Viking Press, 1967), ch. 7. The Olympic revival was suggested by Thomas Bland Hollis; see Samuel Eliot Morison and Henry Steele Commager, *The Growth of the American Republic* (New York: Oxford University Press, 1942), p. 321.

32. On Hamilton's opposition to the use of ancient exemplars: Harvey Flaumenhaft, "Hamilton on the Foundation of Government," *The Political Science Reviewer* 6 (Fall 1976): 152-58.

33. Frederick Rudolph, ed., *Essays on Education in the Early Republic: Benjamin Rush, Noah Webster, Robert Coram, Simeon Doggett, Samuel Harrison Smith, Amable-Louis-Rose de Lafitte du Courteil, Samuel Knox* (Cambridge: Harvard University Press, 1965.)

34. Franklin's "Proposals," p. 138, nn. 12–13; pp. 145 ff., from Locke, *Thoughts*, 168.

35. Rudolph, ed., *Essays on Education*, pp. 18 ff., pp. 45 ff.

36. Frederick Rudolph, *The American College and University: A History* (New York: Vintage Books, 1962), ch. 12.

37. Du Pont de Nemours's pronouncement is revealing: "All our great men have overcome the misfortune of having gone through these studies" (Pierre Samuel du Pont de Nemours, *National Education in the United States of America*, B. G. du Pont, trans. [Newark: University of Delaware Press, 1923], p. 124; see also Francis Wayland's "Report to the Corporation of Brown University, 1850," in *The Colleges and the Public*, Classics in Education no. 15, pp. 135 ff.).

38. Mayo, *op. cit.*, p. 345.

39. Edwin T. Martin, *Thomas Jefferson: Scientist*, (New York: Henry Schuman, 1952), p. 44; for the quarrel with mathematics in the interests of observational science, see Debus, *Science and Education in the Seventeenth Century*, p. 39.

40. Ticknor's efforts: Richard Hofstadter and Wilson Smith, eds., *American Higher Education: A Documentary History* (Chicago: The University of Chicago Press, 1961), pt. 4, nos. 2, 3, 6, 8, 9. Developments after Civil War: Rudolph, *American College and University*, ch. 13.

41. See Jean Le Rond d'Alembert, *Preliminary Discourse to the Encyclopedia of Diderot*, Richard N. Schwab, ed. (Indianapolis: The Library of Liberal Arts, The Bobbs-Merrill Company, 1963), pp. 47, 76; the "tree of sciences" in Bacon: *Advancement*, II, v. 2; *Novum Organum* I, 79; see also George B. Watts, "Thomas Jefferson, the 'Encyclopédie' and the 'Encyclopédie Méthodique'," *French Review* 38 (January 1965): p. 319.

42. For Madison, the constitutional issue was certainly the first consideration. It is a sign of the stature of these men that both (but particularly Madison) worked to supply the students with a theological library for extracurricular reading; see David E. Swift, "Thomas Jefferson, John Holt Rice and Education in Virginia, 1815–25," *Journal of Presbyterian History* 49, no. 1 (Spring 1971): 44–46.

43. Rudolph, *American College and University*, p. 54.

44. du Pont de Nemours, *National Education*, p. 124.

45. Destutt de Tracy, *A Treatise on Political Economy, to which is Prefixed a Supplement to a Preceding Work on the Understanding, or Elements of Ideology* (Georgetown: 1817; reprinted by the Detroit Center for Health Education); Adrienne Koch, *The Philosophy of Thomas Jefferson* (New York: Columbia University Press, 1943), pp. 64–82; Ideology as zoology, p. 67.

46. Lawrence A. Cremin, *American Education: The Colonial Experience, 1607–1783* (New York: Harper and Row, 1970), p. 383.

47. Metaphysical disputations: James J. Walsh, *Education of the Founding Fathers of the Republic; Scholasticism in the Colonial Colleges* (New York: Fordham University Press, 1935), p. 294; on the difficulty of making a place for science in the humanistic curriculum, see Thomas H. Huxley, *Science and Education* (New York: Greenwood Press, 1968; first published in 1898), p. 141 and passim. The bald claim that science is *the* knowledge worth having and *the* proper object of education had been made by Spencer (*Herbert Spencer on Education*, Classics in Education no. 30, Andreas M. Kazamias, ed., pp. 129 ff.).

48. Morrill is quoted in Rudolph, *American College and University*, p. 249; the second quotation is from Jacques Barzun, "The Ivory Lab," Esther Kronovet and Evelyn Shirk, eds., *In Pursuit of Awareness* (New York: Appleton-Century-Crofts, 1967), p. 436.

49. For Jefferson's early reading: Gilbert Chinard, ed., *The Commonplace Book of Thomas Jefferson, A Repository of His Ideas of Government* (Baltimore, The Johns Hopkins Press, 1926).

50. During the presidential campaign of 1800 there were clerical attacks on his personal life, especially his cohabitation with the slave Sally Hemmings at Monticello. There were also damaging imputations of atheism. See Fred C. Luebke, "The Origins of Jefferson's Anti-Clericalism," *Church History* 32 (September 1963): 344 ff. Clerical opposition also frustrated Jefferson's eagerly pursued appointment of Thomas Cooper, a staunch materialist, to the chair of physical science at the University.

51. See Bolingbroke, *On Reticence in Criticism, A Letter to Alexander Pope* for "Pythagorean and Platonic Whimsies." Jefferson's *Literary Bible*, Chinard, ed., contains a high proportion of Bolingbroke selections; see especially p. 55; on Plato in the Enlightenment, see Peter Gay, *The Enlightenment: An Interpretation* (New York: Alfred A. Knopf, 1966), I, 83.

52. Rudolph, ed., *Essays on Education*, p. 178.

53. David Little, "The Origins of Perplexity: Civil Religion and Moral Belief in the Thought of Thomas Jefferson," *American Civil Religion* (New York: Harper and Row, 1974), p. 200.

54. Letter to Charles Pinkney, 4 March 1801.

55. David Tyack, "Forming the National Character: Paradox in the Educational Thought of the Revolutionary Generation," *Harvard Educational Review* 36, no. 1 (Winter 1966): 37.

56. La Fontainerie, *French Liberalism*, passim.

57. For the quality of their learning, see Hannah Arendt, *On Revolution* (New York: The Viking Press, 1965), p. 221.

58. As distinct from history regarded as a source of examples and warnings, such as Jefferson recommends. Hegel terms such historical reflections *pragmatical*. (*Philosophy of History*, Intro., I, 2.)

59. Hofstadter and Smith, *Documentary History* I, 93–94.

60. Wilhelm von Humboldt, *Humanist Without Portfolio, An Anthology of the Writings of Wilhelm von Humboldt*, Marianne Cowen, trans. (Detroit: Wayne State University Press, 1963), pp. 132–133.

61. Theodore Rawson Crane, ed., *The Colleges and the Public*, Classics in Education no. 15, (1963), pp. 94, 89.

62. *Third Day, On Local Motion*, "Uniform Motion."

63. See *Euclid's Elements* I, pp. 1–5. The quotation occurs in Aristotle commentators; see Liddell and Scott, *Greek-English Lexicon (ageometrḗtos)*.

64. C. P. Snow, "The Two Cultures" (1959), in *The Two Cultures: And a Second Look* (New York: Mentor Books, 1963), pp. 9–26. The infelicity consists in calling these dichotomic degeneracies "cultures" and in defining the scientific branch as having, and the literary branch as not having, "the future in its bones."

65. Edmund Husserl, *The Crisis of European Sciences and Transcendental Phenomenology*, David Carr, trans. (Evanston: Northwestern University Press, 1970), especially App. 6, "The Origin of Geometry," pp. 353 ff; Jacob Klein, *Greek Mathematical Thought and the Origin of Algebra*, Eva Brann, trans. (Cambridge: The M.I.T. Press, 1968; first published in 1934), especially ch. 9; Klein, "Phenomenology and the History of Science," *Philosophical Essays in Memory of Edmund Husserl* (Cambridge: Harvard University Press, 1940), pp. 143–163.

66. For earlier occurrences, see *The Metalogicon of John of Salisbury, A Twelfth Century Defense of the Verbal and Logical Arts of the Trivium*, Daniel D. McGarry, trans. (Berkeley: University of California Press, 1962), p. 167, n. 190.

67. Adrienne Koch, "Pragmatic Wisdom and the American Enlightenment," *The William and Mary Quarterly* 18, no. 3 (1961): 329; for the intensity philosophical communities have been capable of in America, see George Santayana, *Character and Opinion in the United States*, ch. 2.

68. Schelling's *Lectures on the Method of On University Studies* (1803) is, however, an example of the educational interpretation of a system (radical idealism) so strenuous as to appear idiosyncratic. See F. W. J. von Schelling, *On University Studies*, E. S. Morgan, trans. (Athens: Ohio University Press, 1966).

69. See, for example, Hans-Georg Gadamer, *Wahrheit und Methode, Grundzuege einer philosophischen Hermeneutik*, 2d ed. (Tuebingen: J. C. B. Mohr, 1965), particularly the Appendix "Hermeneutik und Humanismus," pp. 477 ff. (English version: *Truth and Method* [New York: Seabury Press, 1975]).

70. John of Salisbury, *Metalogicon* I, 12.

71. *Euclid's Elements* I, 415.

CHAPTER 3

1. For example, Milton interpreted the first Fall as consisting essentially of the introduction into the world of *science—the* schismatic, dividing activity. The Serpent, who has partaken of the forbidden "sapiential sap" of the Tree of Knowledge, seduces Eve by showing her that he yet lives

And knows, and speaks, and reasons, and discerns,
Irrational till then. (*Paradise Lost*, IX, 765.)

So also on the secular side, Heidegger regards the false departure to have been made at the first origin of the tradition, with the very coming into being of metaphysics. (*Nietzsche*, II, viii, "Metaphysics as the History of Being" [1931].) As for the understanding of modernity that sees it as a culminating stage in human advancement, all the Founders subscribed to it; its most unabashed and explicit European proponent, who influenced Jefferson especially, was Condorcet; see his *Sketch for a Historical Picture of the Progress of the Human Mind*.

The modern defenders of the ancients in the long "Battle Between the Ancients and the Moderns," on the other hand, usually maintain the notion of modernity as a corrupting *new* departure which is, however, in part a resurrection of choices rejected in antiquity, in part a secular perversion of Christianity. It goes without saying that my own inquiry takes a middle ground in interpreting modernity as a ruptured continuation, at once debilitating and invigorating, of the ancient tradition.

2. In fact, Tocqueville's contention that the Americans acquire this method without benefit of books, by mere force of democratic circumstance, would argue the other way: that it is democracy that gives rise to an appropriate philosophy. Temporally speaking, however, it does seem significant that the author who mediates in time between the inception of the method and its realization, John Locke, is the one who composed deeply related founding works both of philosophy *and* of politics.

3. Translators of Tocqueville split the difference by introducing allusions both to the Cartesian *Rules for the Direction of the Mind* and the Lockean *Conduct of the Understanding* into their versions of his first sentence, which says that Americans "dirigent leur esprit de la même manière et le conduisent d'après les mêmes règles."

Jefferson's youthful reading was chiefly among the English and Scottish authors; in his late studies he preferred the French developers of the Enlightenment, who were making simplifying corrections of Descartes, particularly in replacing the "two incomprehensibilities" of the Cartesian dual substances, mind and extension, by the single one of thinking matter, and by converting the Cartesian dictum "I think, therefore I am" into "I feel, therefore I am." (Jefferson to Adams, 15 August 1820. The revised Cartesian formula comes from Destutt de Tracy's *Elements of Ideology*; Jefferson never mentions its Cartesian origin, but Tracy does.)

Actually, Jefferson's reading in modern philosophy went back even to those sixteenth-century roots Tocqueville mentions, for he discovered in Charron (a French humanist whose work *Of Wisdom* he admired as "the best treatise on moral philosophy ever written") the original of the Baconian division of faculties (and incidentally of his own list of cardinal virtues, which is, of course, ultimately Socratic: Prudence, Justice, Fortitude, Temperance; to Short, 31

October 1819; see Adrienne Koch, "Pragmatic Wisdom and the American Enlightenment," *The William and Mary Quarterly* 18, no. 3 (1961): 327.). I imagine that what Jefferson admired in Charron was precisely the root characteristic of the Enlightenment, the revolt against the authority of the ancients and the teaching that each person "must assent and yield up his Mind to none, but Reason only," Pierre de Charron, *Of Wisdom*, George Stanhope, trans. (London: Tonson and others, 1729), preface.

4. Clinton Rossiter, *The Political Thought of the American Revolution* (New York: Harcourt, Brace and World, Inc., 1963), pp. 211-212.

5. For a circumscription of this mode of political thought, see Michael Oakeshott, *Rationalism in Politics, and Other Essays* (New York: Basic Books, 1962), pp. 1-13; also Max Weber, *The Protestant Ethic and the Rise of Capitalism*.

6. Hegel, *Encyclopedia of the Philosophical Sciences* 23, gives a critique of the expression *self-thinking* as a pleonasm, here regarding it, of course, not merely as a revealing Enlightenment phrase, but in relation to the true nature of thought.

7. Hegel, who gives in the *Phenomenology of the Spirit* the deepest, because dialectically cogent, review of the Enlightenment, uses language similar to Jefferson's: "The communication of pure insight [that is, the mode of rationality] is therefore comparable to a quiet expansion or to *diffusion*, as of a pure scent in an unresistant atmosphere." (VI, B, ii, a, "Enlightenment.")

8. Locke, *The Second Treatise of Civil Government*, ch. 8: "It is necessary the body should move that way whither the greater force carries it, which is the consent of the majority."

9. Above all, the Kantian *Critique of Pure Reason* presents the subject as supplying the form and receiving the material of its objects. On the dominance of the *subject* in modern times, and on the conversion of the ancient *hypokeimenon* into a modern *subjectum*, as well as the rise of a correlative *objectum*, see Heidegger, *Nietzsche*, II, v: "The Dominance of the Subject in Modernity"; viii: "The Transformation of the *Hypokeimenon* into the *Subjectum*." The school use of the word *subject*, meaning *subject-matter* evidently goes back to the classical meaning of *subjectum*: that which underlies what is predicated, that which speech is about.

10. Jacques Barzun, *The House of Intellect* (New York: Harper Torchbooks, 1959), p. 15 and note, for a critique and sample of the uses of the word *creativity*. It is significant that *spontaneity* was originally regarded as the peculiar characteristic, not of feeling but of thought, that is, it is the capacity thought has of originating itself (Kant, *Critique*, B 75).

11. Justin Buchler, *The Concept of Method* (New York: Columbia University Press, 1961), p. 125. The following passage is also to the point: "Many things pass for 'theory' in political science. Among other things, 'theory' may refer to a set of categories that constitutes an 'approach' or 'conceptual scheme,' or, at a more sophisticated level, theory may consist of a set of statements that specify relationships among variables tending toward deter-

minacy." It is from *Contemporary Political Analysis*, James C. Charlesworth, ed. (New York: The Free Press, 1967), pp. 187–88.

12. Tocqueville wisely cites Pascal, and significantly *not* Descartes, as an example of this love.

13. Jefferson to Adams, 14 March 1820: "I confess I should, with Mr. Locke, prefer swallowing one incomprehensibility rather than two. It requires one effort only to admit the single incomprehensibility of matter endowed with thought." The reference is apparently to Locke's *Essay*, IV, 3, 6.

14. A further Jeffersonian example of reason considered as revelation: He explains Socrates' "Daemon" by observing, "He probably considered the suggestion of his . . . reason, as revelation," and approves Adams's suggestion that "the human understanding is a revelation from its maker." (To Adams, 12 October 1813.) The phrase about ignorance being "the softest pillow on which man can rest his head," which Jefferson repeats in respect to his "estrangement" from politics, is attributed by him to Montaigne. (To Edmund Randolph, 3 February 1794; Montaigne, "Of Experience.")

15. Hans-Georg Gadamer, *Wahrheit und Methode, Grundzuege einer philosophischen Hermeneutik*, 2d ed. (Tuebingen, J. C. B. Mohr, 1965), pp. 56 ff., the sections on "Erlebnis," which deal with the literary structuring of "experiences."

16. Jefferson's favorite, Charron, devotes a chapter to the "Seat or Instrument" of the faculty of the reason, relocating it from its ancient place, the heart, in the brain or head (ancient exception: Plato *Timaeus* 73d). That is the physical counterpart to the philosophical reversal of their functions. (*Of Wisdom*, I, xiii; see note 3.)

17. In Locke's *Thoughts* (8) the word *emotion* is still the merely physical state of something that has been set in motion, like blood after exercise. The modern use indicates an affection both turbulent and in need of expression.

18. The head-heart dichotomy is set out, particularly in respect to the students of the decade of the sixties, by Theodore Roszak in *The Making of a Counter Culture; Reflections on the Technocratic Society and Its Youthful Opposition* (Garden City: Anchor Books, 1969), pp. 76 ff.

19. Wilson Smith, ed., *Theories of Education, in Early America 1655-1819* (Indianapolis: The Bobbs-Merrill Company, 1973), p. 132.

20. Recall Jefferson's deprecation of morality as a school subject, with which he logically connects an attack on Wollaston's "most whimsical" theory that truth is the foundation of morality. (To Carr, 10 August 1787; to Law, 13 June 1814.) But without the warrant of some such theory morality is surely formally unteachable.

21. The reason and the passions may even be related as form to material, as when the passions are understood to be the *materialized reasons* of the soul, that is, embodied psychic motives (*logio enyloi*: Aristotle, *On the Soul* I, 403 a.)

22. This ordinary use is opposed to that other traditional one, deriving from

Plato and Aristotle, in which the form is the *essence* of a thing. The phrase *condition of possibility* is Kantian (*Critique of Pure Reason* A III.), though, to be sure, for Kant the formal constituent, that is, the conceiving activity of consciousness, does give a thing, that is, an object, its essence, albeit an attenuated one.

23. Bacon: *Advancement*, II, xxv, 6; he calls for this inquiry as a kind of divine dialectic. Locke, *Essay*, I, 1, 7; the "secure possession of truths" that most concern us is impossible "whilst we let loose our thought into the vast ocean of Being." Kant: *The Limits of Sense and Reason* (Letter to Herz, 21 February 1772) was an early title for the *Critique of Pure Reason*, which contains that very dialectic demanded by Bacon. Kant, of course, refers to Hume, that "geographer of the human reason," as the drawer of the "horizons" Locke demands. (*Critique*, B 788.)

24. Jacob Klein, *Greek Mathematical Thought and the Origin of Algebra*, Eva Brann, trans. (Cambridge: The M.I.T. Press, 1968; first published in 1934), pp. 207 ff.

25. See *The Supreme Court and Education*, Classics in Education no. 4, pp. 3-124, passim. The fundamental American statement on religious freedom is Madison's *Memorial and Remonstrance Against Religious Assessments* (1785), which makes precisely the point that *because* homage to the Creator is a private duty, before and beyond civil society, "Religion is wholly exempt from its cognizance." The *Remonstrance* is cited over and over by the Supreme Court, but particularly in the dissent to *Everson* v. *Board of Education* (1947).

26. The understanding of *pursuit* as a kind of chase is the popular one; in Jefferson's day the term was likely to refer to a profession plied, as in the *pursuit of studies*; see Arthur M. Schlesinger, "The Lost Meaning of 'The Pursuit of Happiness'," *A Casebook on the Declaration of Independence*, Robert Ginsberg, ed. (New York: Thomas Y. Crowell Company, 1967), pp. 216-18. What Tocqueville terms the *melancholy* of the pursuit, whose consummation is *success* rather than happiness, is chronicled in the various sad "Rise of ——" novels like Howell's *The Rise of Silas Lapham*, and Cahan's *The Rise of David Levinsky*.

27. "A mere etymologist is the very lowest character in the republick of letters," says John Clarke, in *Letters to a Student in the University of Cambridge, Massachusetts* (Boston: Samuel Hall, 1796), p. 46. The lowest character perhaps, but also one of the most indispensable for the interpretation of texts. Incidentally, this series of fourteen letters, by a minister to a Harvard freshman, presents an unusual case in early republican writing: a description of a liberal education that happily combines the classical with the modern curriculum—ancient languages with mathematics and science, the "metaphysical speculations" of Locke and Reid with theology. Reid's "Common Sense" dominated American academic philosophy in the early nineteenth century. Henry F. May, *The Enlightenment in America* (New York: Oxford University Press, 1976), pp. 344 ff.

28. Ambrose Wathen, "Monastic *Lectio*: Some Clues from Terminology," *Monastic Studies: On Education* no. 12 (Michaelmas 1976): 211-13.

29. See Heidegger, *Being and Time*, I, 2.

30. The indispensable text for this inquiry is Socrates' telling of Diotima's discourse on Eros and philosophy in the Platonic *Symposium* (198 b ff.); note the occasional playful reminders that *love* in the accusative case (*erota*) and *to ask a question* (*erotan*) look alike in Greek; see *Cratylos* 398 d.

31. On the sightlike and senselike character of the intellect (Greek: *nous*) and its activity, see especially Aristotle, *Protrepticus, A Reconstruction*, Anton-Hermann Chroust, ed. (Notre Dame: University of Notre Dame Press, 1964), Fragment 22; and *On the Soul*, III, 426-27.

32. Nature (*physis*) means *growth* in Greek. The word is etymologically connected with the verb *to be*. The first object of "theory" was the heavens. (Plato, *Timaeus* 90 d; Aristotle, *Metaphysics* 982 a.)

Index